AUTISM
EQUALITY
IN THE
WORKPLACE

of related interest

Asperger's Syndrome Workplace Survival Guide
A Neurotypical's Secrets for Success
Barbara Bissonnette
ISBN 978 1 84905 943 5
eISBN 978 0 85700 807 7

The Complete Guide to Getting a Job for People with Asperger's Syndrome
Find the Right Career and Get Hired
Barbara Bissonnette
ISBN 978 1 84905 921 3
eISBN 978 0 85700 692 9

Asperger Syndrome and Employment
What People with Asperger Syndrome Really Really Want
Sarah Hendrickx
ISBN 978 1 84310 677 7
eISBN 978 1 84642 879 1

AUTISM EQUALITY IN THE WORKPLACE

REMOVING BARRIERS AND CHALLENGING DISCRIMINATION

JANINE BOOTH

FOREWORD BY
JOHN MCDONNELL MP

Jessica Kingsley *Publishers*
London and Philadelphia

First published in 2016
by Jessica Kingsley Publishers
73 Collier Street
London N1 9BE, UK
and
400 Market Street, Suite 400
Philadelphia, PA 19106, USA

www.jkp.com

Library of Congress Cataloging in Publication Data
Names: Booth, Janine.
Title: Autism equality in the workplace : removing barriers and challenging discrimination / Janine Booth.
Description: Philadelphia : Jessica Kingsley Publishers, 2016. | Includes bibliographical references and index.
Identifiers: LCCN 2015039415 | ISBN 9781849056786 (alk. paper)
Subjects: LCSH: People with disabilities--Employment. | Autism.
Classification: LCC HV1568 .B666 2016 | DDC 331.5/94-- dc23 LC record available at http://lccn.loc.gov/2015039415

British Library Cataloguing in Publication Data
A CIP catalogue record for this book is available from the British Library

ISBN 978 1 84905 678 6
eISBN 978 1 78450 197 6

Printed and bound in the United States

Contents

Chapter 3

Remove those Barriers! 61

Chapter 4

Autism, Work and the Law 96

Chapter 5

Organising for Change. 109

Foreword

Some years ago the secretary of a local trade union branch approached me, asking for my assistance as the local MP. He didn't want to explain the problem on the telephone and requested a face-to-face meeting. I thought that he'd be coming to see me about a problem his members were having at work or a campaign his union was waging.

In fact, when we met, it was an extremely moving experience as he explained that he had come to see me in desperation about the problems his daughter was experiencing. She was in her late twenties and only a year earlier had been assessed as having Asperger's Syndrome. She was an endearing, bright young woman who had gone through school and early adult life undiagnosed.

Sometimes, when her behaviour did not conform to what others expected, she became confused and stressed at the way people reacted to her. Without any support or professional advice the family was struggling to cope and felt increasingly distressed for her.

This was my first experience as a local MP in undertaking the long, arduous task of gaining recognition of the needs of people on the autistic spectrum in my constituency and securing for them the services and support that they require.

It has been heartrending at times to witness the struggle families have had just to exercise their basic right to gain a professional assessment and to access even basic support services.

As a result I have become active in local and national campaigns to raise awareness of autism. I joined the All Party

Group on Autism in Parliament and lobbied for new legislation to enact new legal rights for people on the autistic spectrum so that they can access the support they need and not be discriminated against.

Through my involvement with the trade union RMT, as the chair of its Parliamentary Group of MPs, I met Janine Booth. Janine was the first trade unionist to raise within the trade union movement and had the brilliant idea of convening training seminars for trade union representatives to improve their understanding of autism and to equip them with the knowledge and resources to overcome the difficulties many people on the autistic spectrum face at work.

I attended the first seminars Janine convened. They were a revelation as people told their own stories of what they had witnessed or experienced themselves in their workplaces. There were some heartbreaking accounts of discrimination, unfairness, ignorance and, worst of all, bullying.

The trade union representatives came away from the seminars with a significantly greater knowledge and understanding of autism. More importantly, they went back to their places of employment with the information and the skills they needed to represent and offer advice and support to their members who either were on the autistic spectrum or had family members who were. Thanks to Janine's work, a cohort of trade union shop stewards and officials are now challenging the discrimination that people experience at work as a result of ignorance and prejudice relating to autism.

This book is Janine's next major contribution to challenging the disadvantages autistic people can suffer at work. It serves as an invaluable guide to the way in which we can transform the workplace so that discrimination against people on the spectrum can be overcome. It is a pioneering piece of work that will both inspire and empower us all to secure the equality at work we aspire to.

John McDonnell MP

Acknowledgements

I am grateful to all the autistic people whom I interviewed for this book. Where there is no endnote otherwise, quotes are from these interviews, using just their first names, some of which have been changed on their request. Autistic and other disabled people have many well-intentioned people and organisations that speak for us, but they do not always say what we want to say. Speaking for ourselves and through our own organisations is key to tackling the misconceptions and the discrimination that we face.

Thanks also to Monica Gort for encouraging and facilitating the 'Autism in the Workplace' training courses that I run, to the late Bob Crow for agreeing to the RMT union sponsoring the courses, and to the many trade union representatives who have attended them and who take the knowledge and skills that they learn back to the workplace to fight inequality. This book develops and updates the ideas that I first set out in the *Autism in the Workplace* handbook published online by the (British) Trade Union Congress in May 2014. I am indebted to Asha Wije, formerly of Simpson Millar, for contributing her legal expertise to the training courses, the handbook and this book. Thanks to Cassie Fox for suggesting that I develop the handbook into the book you are now reading. Finally, thanks to my family for their tolerance and support.

Poem: Manifesto from Behind the Mask

Make me a mask so that no-one can see
That the face that I'm wearing is not really me
Get me a glaze to go over my eyes
To look like I'm looking while melting inside

Fetch me some specs that can read between lines
Fit me antennae that pick up the signs
Lend me a lens that reads unwritten rules
Bless me with patience to help suffer fools

Find me a babel fish trained to translate
The looks and the hints and the traps and the bait
Arm me with ammo so I'm never caught
In the crossfire of banter without a retort

Fit me a filter to sift out distraction
Teach me a trick to predict a reaction
Create me a coat like the back of a duck
So nothing will stick when they throw enough muck

Install me a switch that will turn off my thinking
Considering, probing, deciphering, linking
At least fit a dimmer or slow-mo or pause
To turn down the volume or close all the doors

Give me that gift that they call 'inhibition'
So I know when to hush and reserve my position
Programme an app that decodes all the crap
Build me a bridge 'cross the processing gap

Alternatively…

Make me a world where not every place
Is buzzing with noise or invading my space
Set up society so you can converse
And I can obsess and neither is worse

Where statements are clear and where reasoning's sound
Where some holes are square 'cos not all pegs are round
Where life on a spectrum is not to be feared
Diversity's normal and no-one is weird

Ditch the requirement for all to conform
Broaden our meaning of what is the norm
Change the arrangements, compete rather less
Co-operate more, re-envision 'success'

Where a living's a right not a gift or a perk
Where we're working to live, we're not living to work
Where skills are acknowledged and talents are freed
From each by ability, to each by need

Design a fresh start where there's room to relax
To think, to imagine, to heal up the cracks
Agree some new rules where we all have control
Of our workplaces, life spaces, world as a whole

A future where fear, hate and bullying stop
A system where people not profit come top
Surely this isn't too much that I ask
But until we achieve it – please make me that mask

(Janine Booth 2015)

Introduction

Autistic people experience systematic disadvantage and discrimination in the world of work. This book is about challenging that.

Autistic people and our families and friends have known this through bitter experience for a long time. More recently, the media have been noticing, governments have issued strategies, and statistics have been appearing. Chapter 1 of this book begins with a graphic presentation of some of those statistics and continues with a discussion of some commonly held views about autism, particularly regarding work: are they myths, realities or both?

This is by no means the first book about autism and employment but I believe that it takes a new and radical approach. Many existing books advise autistic people how to adapt, how to behave, how to fit in, how to get into a job and survive there. This advice can be very useful but it is not enough.

This book does not advise autistic people how to change. It calls instead for workplaces to change. It demands that employment fit all workers rather than autistic workers fitting ourselves into an employment structure that is, in large part, distressing, discriminatory and disabling.

For a long time, autism has been understood and explained in terms of impairment. In the 1970s, Dr Lorna Wing introduced the concept of a 'triad of impairments' that all autistic people share: difficulties with social interaction, social communication and social imagination. Although this was a significant step forward in understanding autism at the time, I believe that it has been improved on and even superseded by the approach that views autism as part of human *neurological diversity*.

We are a neurologically diverse species: different people have different neurological make-up, different brain wiring. A significant minority have autistic brain wiring: we are *neuroatypical* or *neurodivergent*. Other minority neurological conditions include dyslexia, dyspraxia and attention deficit hyperactivity disorder. People who do not have one of these conditions are *neurotypical*.

Autistic educator Nick Walker (2014a) explains that:

Neurodiversity is a natural and valuable form of human diversity...the idea that there is one 'normal' or 'healthy' type of brain or mind, or one 'right' style of neurocognitive functioning, is a culturally constructed fiction, no more valid...than the idea that there is one 'normal' or 'right' ethnicity, gender or culture.

Together with the social model of disability (outlined in Chapter 1), this approach allows us to develop a strategy to change workplaces rather than workers.

So this book will not list the characteristics of autism and explain the problems that each of them causes at work. Rather, it will look at the barriers that workplaces create for autistic people (in Chapter 2) and measures to remove those barriers (in Chapter 3). Along the way, this will explain a lot about autism and about the experience of being autistic in a hostile world.

Chapter 4 provides a guide to relevant legislation. It outlines international legal principles and gives a concise guide to ten key legal concepts. One of those concepts is 'reasonable accommodations' (called 'reasonable adjustments', i.e. changes to working conditions to enable a disabled worker to do his job, in some countries). The information in this book can help autistic workers to obtain the accommodations they need. However, it would be far better for an autistic worker to arrive at an autism-friendly workplace rather than confronting many distressing factors, identifying each one individually and demanding adjustments. So I advocate that workplaces change without waiting for an identified autistic worker to request a change.

Autism is a spectrum: each person's autism shows itself in different ways and to different degrees. For a few autistic people, perhaps especially those with fewer needs and plentiful resources, relatively simple accommodations may enable them to thrive at work, or at least to thrive as well as their neurotypical workmates. More substantial changes will deliver more substantial benefits but genuine accessibility and equality requires much more radical and thoroughgoing change. Autistic people will remain excluded and disadvantaged until we have a revolution in the way that work is organised: a transformation whereby those doing the work gain control over how it is done, in a way that recognises and accommodates the diverse neurologies of the workforce.

This book aims to be not just a call for change but a handbook for achieving it. So its final chapter sets out a strategy to make change happen. I argue that autistic people and our allies cannot wait for employers, governments or laws to liberate us but can bring about much more rapid and effective progress by our own efforts, alongside and as part of the trade union and disabled people's movements.

To misquote Karl Marx, 'Thus far, autistic people have had to navigate, suffer or avoid the workplace. The point, however, is to change it.'

Chapter 1

Autism in the Workplace

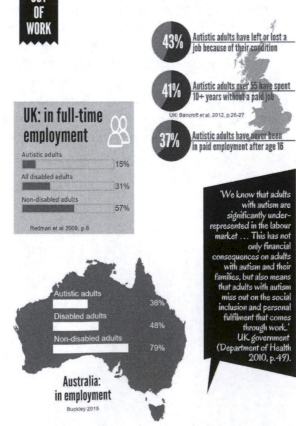

Figure 1.1. Out of work

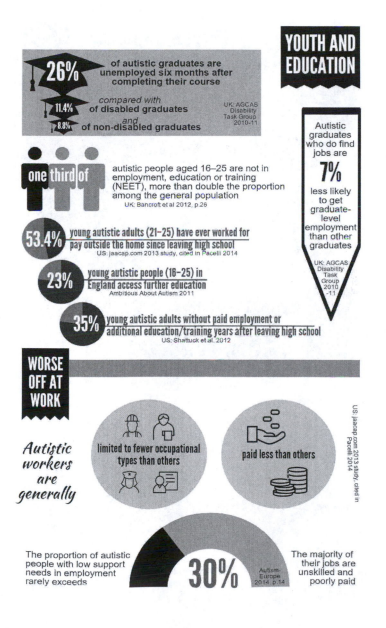

YOUTH AND EDUCATION

26% of autistic graduates are unemployed six months after completing their course

compared with
11.4% of disabled graduates

and
8.8% of non-disabled graduates

UK: AGCAS Disability Task Group 2010-11

Autistic graduates who do find jobs are **7%** less likely to get graduate-level employment than other graduates

UK: AGCAS Disability Task Group 2010-11

one third of autistic people aged 16–25 are not in employment, education or training (NEET), more than double the proportion among the general population
UK: Bancroft et al 2012, p.26

53.4% young autistic adults (21–25) have ever worked for pay outside the home since leaving high school
US: jaacap.com 2013 study, cited in Pacelli 2014

23% young autistic people (16–25) in England access further education
Ambitious About Autism 2011

35% young autistic adults without paid employment or additional education/training years after leaving high school
US: Shattuck et al. 2012

WORSE OFF AT WORK

Autistic workers are generally

limited to fewer occupational types than others

paid less than others

US: jaacap.com 2013 study, cited in Pacelli 2014

The proportion of autistic people with low support needs in employment rarely exceeds **30%**
Autism-Europe 2014 p.14

The majority of their jobs are unskilled and poorly paid

Figure 1.2. Getting a job

Figure 1.3. Youth

MYTHS OR REALITIES?

There is an autism epidemic

There has been a big rise in identified prevalence of autism[1] but this is not the same as a rise in autism. The increase in diagnoses can be explained by increased knowledge of autism, improved diagnostic methods, wider diagnostic criteria, autistic people speaking out and giving a more positive view of life on the spectrum, and the parents of the rising number of children diagnosed as autistic realising that they are autistic too.

It may also be that increasing sensory stimulus and mounting pressure to conform socially, including in the workplace, has caused more difficulty for autistic people, so more of us seek out answers that lead to diagnosis. Figures 1.1, 1.2 and 1.3 on the previous pages show graphically the disadvantaged position of autistic people in employment and society.

Some autistic people are high functioning, some low functioning

People with autism can be very different from each other; some cannot carry out their own personal care, some do not talk, others have no problems in these areas but difficulties in others. The spectrum is not a straight line from 'mild' to 'severe': a person can have low function in some areas but high function in others. One autistic worker may work brilliantly at the technical functions of her job but have woeful timekeeping; another may be scrupulously punctual but struggle to maintain focus without supervision. It is more useful to discuss individuals' needs than to label them high or low functioning.

---

1 For example, the US Autism and Developmental Disabilities Monitoring (ADDM) Network shows a rise in prevalence among children, from 1 in 150 in 2000 to 1 in 68 in 2015 (www.cdc.gov/ncbddd/autism/data.html, accessed 30 November 2015).

AUTISM EQUALITY IN THE WORKPLACE

Autism is a disability

Using the social model of disability, we can see that society disables autistic people. So yes, autistic people are disabled. We are entitled to the support, protections, rights, services and welfare benefits that disabled people have.

However, many autistic people assert that autism is not just or always a disability – it is a *difference* and it has positive aspects that are often overlooked.

Autism is a mental illness

Autism is not in itself a mental illness. Autistic people are more vulnerable to mental health problems due to distress caused by social conflict, sensory overload, discrimination and other factors: the National Autistic Society Scotland (NAS Scotland) estimates that almost one-third of autistic adults develop severe mental health problems due to lack of support (SPICe 2010, p.18). The UK government admits that 'adults with autism and mental health conditions can be at a double disadvantage in the labour market' (Department of Health 2010, p.54).

Autism is a learning disability

Autism is not in itself a learning disability but it can often be accompanied by learning disability. An estimated 35.4 per cent of adults with learning disabilities are autistic (Health and Care Information Centre 2012).

Autism is a disorder

While its official title is 'autistic spectrum disorder', many autistic people prefer the term 'autistic spectrum condition', seeing 'disorder' as a pejorative term – and also an ironic one, given the highly ordered thinking characteristic of autism. Autistic educator Nick Walker (2014b) argues: 'Ultimately, to describe autism as a disorder represents a value judgment rather than a scientific fact.'

Autistic people are of low intelligence

No. Autism is a spectrum and includes people across the range of intelligence.

Most autistic people are male

Many more boys and men than girls and women are diagnosed as autistic. The UK's NHS estimates that 2.0 per cent of men and 0.3 per cent of women have an autistic spectrum condition (Health and Care Information Centre 2012). However, diagnosis is geared more towards how autistic traits show in males; girls may be more likely to mask their autistic traits than boys; girls wait longer than boys for a diagnosis and are more likely to be misdiagnosed (Bancroft et al. 2012, p.11).

Without further research and while our society still constructs 'maleness' and 'femaleness' beyond actual physical differences, we will not know whether women are really less likely to be autistic or whether the pathway to diagnosis is more clearly signposted for men.

Work is good for autistic people

Certainly, impoverished unemployment is not good for autistic people. The UK's Autism Strategy acknowledges that 'the ability to get, and keep, a job and then to progress in work is the best route out of poverty, and a central part of social inclusion' (Department of Health 2010, p.49).

However, research shows that having a job does not necessarily lead autistic adults to live more independently (Autism-Europe 2014, p.20) and that where and how autistic people work affects their wellbeing (Heasley 2014).

Coercive policies that force autistic people into unsuitable jobs will not benefit them, even if they improve the employment figures. Autism-Europe (2014, p.44) states bluntly: 'To subject a person to situations that are highly stressful or even completely overwhelming for them, without adequate support, when this can be avoided, can be dangerous for the individual and can also be regarded as an abusive practice.'

Most autistic people can't work in normal workplaces

Many autistic people can work, including in 'normal' (whatever that means!) workplaces – unless it is considered 'normal' to exclude autistic workers!

This book identifies factors that make it difficult for autistic adults to work, such as unsuitable working conditions, bullying, discrimination or a lack of reasonable adjustments, and argues that if these were changed, more autistic people could work.

There are no autistic people where I work

How do you know? You can't tell just by looking! You might have colleagues who do not know they are autistic or who do not want to tell you.

Autistic people have extraordinary special talents

While some people on the autistic spectrum have unusual, striking abilities, it is unfair to expect all autistic people to be like this, or to treat their abilities like 'party tricks'. Moreover, it does not mean that they do not face other barriers.

We now have what I'd call 'the Bill Gates problem'. People now have an idea of autistic people having special talents. People look at my profile and say they can't believe I'm out of work and when I say I have Asperger's, they say that in my field that should be an asset. Maybe it should, but maybe they are not aware of the difficulties and barriers put in our way. (Lauren, civil service scientist)

Autistic people have lots of skills to offer employers

The National Autistic Society and UK government publication *Untapped Talent* (Department for Work and Pensions and National Autistic Society 2012) lists skills that autistic people may have: problem solving, attention to detail, concentration, reliability, loyalty, technical ability, specialist skills and interests, detailed factual knowledge, excellent memory, job retention and resourcefulness.

In the document's foreword, government minister Lord Freud (who became notorious for supporting a suggestion that some disabled people might be paid less than the minimum wage) argued that businesses becoming autism friendly is 'about tapping into and seeking out the most talented individual for a role'. As he does not mention hiring less talented people, it appears that Freud is recommending to businesses that they 'cherry-pick' those autistic workers with the highest skill levels.

Autistic people are computer nerds; they excel at technical, not creative, things

Autism diagnosis in Silicon Valley is at twice the average level (European Disability Forum 2014). Many autistic people excel at the technical (and solo) working involved but there are many talented autistic artists and performers too, some of whom I spoke to for this book. Autism is not a block to creativity.

Singer Lauren Lovejoy says, 'If I didn't have Asperger's I might not be as creative as I am now' (Wheeler 2015b).

Employers should hire autistic people because they are hard-working geniuses who do what they're told without complaining

While it is unacceptable not to employ people because of their autism, it is also unacceptable to see them as easy to exploit.

Moreover, if employers take on only those autistic workers whom they calculate will enhance their profits, they may overlook autistic people with higher support needs.

Autistic people are weirdos with no social skills and are difficult to work with

Social interaction can be problematic for autistic people. Does that mean that autistic people are difficult to work with, or that others are difficult for autistic people to work with? Working together is an issue for everyone and is not helped by narrow views of 'social skills' centred on neurotypicality, which prevent autistic people from receiving support for their social interactions and that detract from employers' responsibility to engage with them.

Autism is just an excuse for bad or antisocial behaviour

'Bad behaviour' can just be unusual or eccentric behaviour, which may not harm anyone. Behaviour that does cause difficulties may be the product of distress in a situation that does not take into account the needs of the autistic person.

My autistic colleague has good social skills – I don't see the problem

Your Russian colleague might also speak very good English! For autistic people, social interaction can be like communicating in a foreign language: we usually have to work very hard to develop and maintain our social skills and can find it difficult and tiring.

Autistic people like boring, repetitive work

Repetitive tasks may suit some autistic people some of the time, but it would be wrong to ghettoise or exploit autistic workers by assuming that the dull work can be dumped on them.

> I get the impression that the assumption is that the right way to treat autistic workers is to give them routine, predictable work, and to assume that they have no career ambitions. (Lauren, civil service scientist)

> I left school at 16, and went through a whole succession of jobs, and I could never hold one down. I was largely bored, doing things like working on an assembly line and routine shop work. The first job I had was sticking soles onto shoes. I was sacked after two weeks with a written reason that I worked at a quarter of the speed of everyone else. The job bored me. (Keith, journalist)

APPLYING THE SOCIAL MODEL OF DISABILITY TO AUTISM

There are different ways of understanding disability. The two main ones are:

- the social model
- the medical (or individual) model.

The social model looks at the barriers that our society puts in the way of disabled (in this case, autistic) people's participation. It aims to remove unnecessary barriers that prevent disabled people accessing work and services and living independently.

The social model distinguishes between impairment and disability:

- Impairment is a characteristic or reduction in function.
- Disability is the difficulty experienced by people with an impairment because society is not taking sufficient measures to take account of their needs.

For example, an autistic person's hypersensitivity to bright light may be considered to be an impairment, but the disability is caused by the bright lights in the workplace; the barrier can be removed by turning down the light.

The social model originates from the disabled people's movement of the 1970s, when the medical model was the established way of thinking.

> For a long period, disability was thought by almost everyone to signify an inability to live a 'normal life'. Disabled people were seen as either the pathetic and helpless objects of charity, or else, if they managed, despite everything, to succeed in their careers and lives, as heroic figures overcoming their 'defects' (not, note, the barriers) by superhuman effort. (Trade Union Congress 2015)

During a decade in which many groups rose up to resist the oppression they had long experienced, including gay and women's liberation movements, disabled people rejected the medical model and replaced it with a new way of understanding their position. By arguing that society disables impaired people, the social model turned the traditional view of disability upside down. The distinction between the two is important beyond academic interest. It enables us to understand the nature of disablement in a way that guides practical action. Its application may be more or less complex in practice but its approach is straightforward: first identify barriers, then remove them.

By identifying disabling social barriers to participation and equality, the social model points to what needs to be changed: 'It is about fitting the job to the worker, rather than the worker to the job' (Trade Union Congress 2015). It therefore places the responsibility on government, policymakers and institutions to make changes. In the world of work, this demands that employers and workplaces, rather than autistic workers, must change.

If a workplace or working practice is organised around only one way of doing things, it may be disabling to those workers who do things differently. Autistic worker Victoria (2014) contends: 'In a culture and society more understanding and tolerant of difference, I don't believe many of my differences would even register as "difficulties" in the first place.'

The old thinking that dominated before the disabled people's movement devised the social model has harmed, and continues to harm, autistic people's prospects for equality. Autistic campaigner Damian Milton (2012) argues that together with other factors, the medical model 'has done great damage to autistic people, and takes attention away from the social conditions, and the disadvantaged social position such thinking places autistic people in.' For Kabie Brook of Scotland's Autism Rights Group, Highland, 'Often we are reduced to a dehumanising list of deficits: a problem to be managed rather than real people with lives to live' (Wheeler 2015a).

Autism campaigns and charities advocate the social model of disability. Many governments and agencies have adopted it formally. Many employers' policies state that this is the model they use. However, their practices and their workers' experiences may tell a different story, as some of the testimonies in this book illustrate.

The law has taken some steps towards the social model while still bearing the imprint of the medical model. For example, the obligation on employers to make reasonable adjustments or accommodations echoes the social model's aim of removing barriers but, to make this demand, a worker must first prove that she is disabled by proving what she cannot do: a medical model approach. It identifies accommodations as measures that are necessary because of an individual's deficits. This puts the onus on the individual to come forward; marks her out as different (a self-perception most of us have had all our lives and would rather not have emphasised); misses out individuals who do not come forward, perhaps because they do not know that they are autistic, or do not know their rights or lack the support to assert them; misses the opportunity to use the autistic perspective to improve the workplace for everyone and may provoke a backlash by appearing to give some individuals 'special treatment'.

Further, a broad social model approach would require workplaces to become autism friendly in a general sense, not just to make individual changes in response to demands from individuals. However, government autism strategy notably fails to compel employers to do this. The UK's strategy compels the government and local and health authorities to take certain actions, but not employers. Its 'right to control' (Department of Health 2010, pp.55–56) addresses an individual's choice and control over services, benefits and how she receives them but is silent about any right to control over working conditions.

The social model has its critics, and some doubt that it can be applied successfully to autism. One criticism is that it understates the impact of impairment, the very real difficulties caused to a person by her physical or mental problems. Similarly, there is a concern that the greater impairments of some autistic people may be played down or overlooked relative to those more able to function in society whom it may be easier or more profitable to integrate. Some also doubt that our understanding of autism is sufficient to enable us to identify meaningful barriers.

Our understanding of autism has some way to go but we know enough to make a start. Certainly, many of the barriers to autistic workers are more subtle than those facing other disabled workers: social misunderstanding is less tangible than the obvious barrier of a staircase confronting a wheelchair user.

It is much more complicated and challenging than for other disabilities, because we know that every person with autism is different. You have to be more creative. It requires a lot more explanation and more awareness-raising so that people are aware of the barriers faced by people with autism. It is definitely a challenge, but I don't think we should say that the social model doesn't apply to autism. (Aurélie Baranger, Director, Autism-Europe)

Perhaps, as the popular neurotypical figure of speech goes, the proof of the pudding is in the eating. Let's start to identify those barriers.

Chapter 2

Ten Barriers in the Way of Autistic Workers

1. GETTING WORK

Starting behind the starting line

Barriers stand in the way of autistic people before they even apply for a job. Many of today's autistic adults were undiagnosed autistic children and did not get the support and self-knowledge that comes with diagnosis until later in life:

> I was only diagnosed with Asperger's when I was 41. This came after 20 years of leading with work-related problems that could not be explained at the time or were put down to my 'strange' personality and a profound inability to behave like everyone else in a work environment. (Richard 2013)

> My diagnosis also came too late, my hopes of a career gone as the depression and social anxiety I developed took away my teens and twenties. I'm trying hard to progress but it's taking a huge chunk of my thirties too. (Sarah 2014)

The education system may have failed them, leaving autistic job hunters underqualified and underconfident.

Autism-Europe (2014, p.13) reports that many autistic adults have academic qualifications significantly below their potential and that 'across Europe, there is a widespread lack of vocational training and higher education options that are suited to the needs of adults with autism'.

> Michael had to change schools because of bullying, went to another school and was bullied again. He was in and out of school, and had lots of disruption coming up to his GCSEs. He came out less qualified than he could have been. He went to university, but got no support. He's as bright as his sister or his brother, but he couldn't stay in school because it was an awful environment for him. As a result, he had no self-confidence. (Kate, Michael's sister)

Unsuitable education may be followed by unsuitable employment. A patchy work record makes an unimpressive CV/resumé and knocks confidence.

> I have good qualifications and have had very many jobs. Sadly, work never lasted long due to a combination of anxiety, stress caused by travelling, endemic bullying in the workplace, sensory problems, sleeplessness, etc. I can no longer face the thought of a return to work and feel literally sick at the thought. (Eleni 2013)

Get a job!

Finding the right job is a field laid with mines.

> The biggest obstacle is the lack of support to get a job that is appropriate rather than bureaucratic. Michael's never even seen a specialist disability support worker. Our parents support him, but it would be useful if someone outside the family, a professional, could be involved and liaise with potential employers. With better support, Michael could have found a niche by now. (Kate, Michael's sister)

Louisa (2015) contacted an employment service for autistic adults: 'The waiting list was so long that I ended up landing a job through my own efforts. This proved to be more of a curse than a blessing... I was dismissed just five months into the new job.'

Estimates from several countries claim that 80 per cent of jobs are not advertised publicly (Nishi 2013 is a US example). So job hunters are advised to network. The person who finds it hard to network, who has few contacts, is disadvantaged.

Even where jobs are advertised, the advert can present barriers. It may:

- demand a 'type' of person that an autistic person may feel she is not, for example, someone who is 'friendly' or 'confident'

- use jargon, acronyms or figures of speech

- give no information about the workplace's sensory environment or about support or adjustments available.

According to a US survey (cited in Bissonnette 2013a, p.20), employers' top requirement is teamwork, then verbal communication, decision making and problem-solving skills. Technical knowledge, often an autistic strength and logically the most relevant for doing the job, ranked a lowly seventh.

Interviews and other methods of torture

Having jumped the hurdles to apply for a job, the autistic applicant then faces the daunting barrier of the interview.

There is some recognition that autistic applicants may 'struggle to "sell themselves"' (Department for Work and Pensions and National Autistic Society 2012, p.8). Autistic people may even blame themselves: 'I fall down at interviews' (Charlotte 2013); 'I am useless at interviews' (Julie 2013a); 'I sweated like a pig at interviews, grinned like an idiot and stumbled through questions that to me seemed totally crazy' (Tony 2015).

Perhaps the interview disables the autistic interviewee. How?

- Lack of notice and opportunity to prepare: 'One prospective employer invited me to a workshop, then at the workshop announced that I would be interviewed there and then! I had no chance to prepare and it went really badly' (Josh, data entry assistant).

- Sensory distractions or discomforts, such as bright lights, noise or smells in the interview room.

- Interviewers expecting immediate answers: 'I didn't pass the face-to-face interview. I thought it went well, but they explained that I took too long to process the questions; they had to ask me twice before I answered' (Eleanore, dog groomer).

- Sloppily worded questions and negative judgement of the autistic applicant's literal answer:

  'Can you tell me about your last job?'

  'Yes.'

  'How did you find your last job?'

  'I saw it posted in the JobCentre.'

  'What can you bring to this job?'

  'My briefcase, work boots and packed lunch.'

- Hypothetical, illogical, unclear or irrelevant questions:

  'Where do you see yourself in ten years' time?' (Probably still in London?)

  'What have you got that the other candidates haven't?' (How do I know that when I don't know the other candidates?)

  'What are your hobbies?' (Why do you want to know?)

- Vague questions: 'Tell me about yourself.'

- Intrusive personal or medical questions.

- Judging applicants on social behaviour.

US employment coach Barbara Bissonnette gives the following advice to her autistic clients that:

> Slouching says you are bored... Your gaze indicates what you are thinking about. Looking at your watch or out of the window, or fiddling with objects, are signals that you are distracted... A firm, confident handshake is another basic job readiness skill... Talking too quickly is seen as a sign of nervousness; speaking too softly suggests a lack of confidence. If your volume is too loud, people will read this as a lack of awareness of your surroundings... Monotone speech...communicates low energy and indifference... Language that is too formal or pretentious...will be interpreted as arrogance. (Bissonnette 2013b, p.84)

Wow – all those assumptions, based not on what you say but on how you say it, how you sit or where you look! Every trait listed could indicate autism rather than the negative conclusion to which this hypothetical hirer jumped.

There are even worse experiences than interviews. 'Stress interviews' deliberately intimidate applicants, ostensibly to test how they deal with pressure. 'Psychometric tests' ask multiple-choice personality questions, a process that autistic writer Rudy Simone (2010, p.102) describes as 'like a bouncer at the door of a nightclub who doesn't let us in because we're unfashionable... personality testing is discrimination as blatant as a "whites only" drinking fountain'. This practice has been widely criticised as ineffective and unethical (Spillane 2012).

Other tests may be more relevant to the job but often these test the ability to pass tests rather than the ability to do the job. Robert wants to be a train driver: he knows he can do the job as he drove a train successfully during his apprenticeship and trains have been his special interest from a very young age. But the railway company he works with insists on written rather than practical tests for staff applying to become drivers and Robert failed the tests.

Should an applicant tell a prospective employer that he is autistic? Disclosing autism may allow him to request adjustments and explain unusual behaviour but it may lead to discrimination. Civil servant Austin says: 'My GP said there was a danger in telling employers that I am autistic because employers would have prejudices, like assuming that I would have disruptive behaviour, which I don't.'

2. GETTING ON WITH THE JOB

Having navigated these barriers and got a job, more barriers appear. It takes time for autistic people to adjust to new routines and unfamiliar surroundings. Induction to the job is supposed to assist with this but may:

- not cover aspects of work that non-autistic workers may assume or 'pick up' (e.g. what to do during your break)

- give a large amount of information verbally

- leave workers to 'sink or swim' socially.

Training may not be geared to autistic learning styles. Training in groups may present problems because of processing speed differences, social anxiety and distractions.

I got training from a person who found it difficult to understand my language difficulty, so I was then trained by another person and the training wasn't very good. There was no emphasis on assisting with my disability. (Austin, civil servant)

Beyond the induction, employers may overlook the training of autistic workers:

I never had any provision for further study, only for mandatory things. I have never been seen as worth investing in because I'm the weirdo, the oddball. (Jules, nurse)

Employers may not recognise autistic people's abilities. Charlotte (2013) contacted an employment support scheme: 'All they could supply me with was a lengthy disclosure document to personalise for potential employers, looking more at my weaknesses and needs than my strengths!' Content writer Luke feels so undervalued that he is 'desperate to leave' his job.

Promotion processes present similar barriers to the initial application, creating an autistic 'glass ceiling'. Journalist Keith says that despite excelling at his job, 'In 19 years, I've not been promoted once. The "blue-eyed boys and girls" climbed up the management ladder.'

Help in overcoming these barriers may not be forthcoming, especially if the worker is not diagnosed as autistic: 'My entire school experience and first two jobs happened to somebody who was assumed to be neurotypical… I received no assistance in school or my early employment career' (Jeanette Purkis 2014).

The same difficulty can be experienced by those who feel unable to come out of the autistic closet:

Michael's not out about his Asperger's. He wouldn't dream of telling anyone. So he hasn't had any adjustments made. (Kate, Michael's sister)

I was ashamed of this condition. I never used to tell anybody. People would see it as a weakness and take advantage, or would treat you as a freak or discriminate against you. I thought I was in danger of deterring people. (Austin, civil servant)

3. COMMUNICATION

Autistic and non-autistic people communicate differently. Autistic people are more likely to think, speak and hear literally and to have distinct preferences for a particular medium of communication, whereas non-autistic people are more likely to rely on clues from context, tone, gestures and other factors. Neither way is right or wrong but, as the minority, autistic people usually come off worse from communication clashes. Julie (2013b) says that these mismatches 'can get you a reputation for being a thoroughly awful person, a reputation which is entirely undeserved and which…no-one will ever tell you about.'

Please don't let me be misunderstood

You could probably fill a chapter with anecdotes in which an autistic worker's manager communicates less than clearly with consequences that make for amusing reading but trouble at work: the scheduler told to 'look at' new software, who looked at it and then was admonished for not using it (Bissonnette 2013a, p.22); the engineer bewildered by instructions to 'leverage the brand' and 'give customers a religious experience' (Bissonnette 2013a, p.141); and the story I heard of the Newcastle station assistant, told to 'sweep the Carlisle platform', who travelled to Carlisle station and swept its platform.

Whether in instructions or in workplace rules, lack of clarity is unhelpful and even distressing:

> Some of the briefs forwarded to me by account managers were extremely vague and poorly written. I've tried to work with them but it hasn't always ended well. (Luke, content writer)

> When they refer to 'the track', they don't just mean the track, they mean the whole area around it. Because I take things literally, this is illogical to me. (Syed, railway track engineer)

Colleagues may leave things unsaid – for example, asking you to do some photocopying without telling you what to do with the copies. Alexandra (Brown 2008, p.49) does not know when she is being told something for her information or to act on. Why? Because the person did not tell her.

Or the employer may not tell the worker how his task fits into the overall production process. Maybe the manager assumes that people will just know or do not care but it may be neither obvious nor uninteresting to the autistic worker.

Autistic people may understand written or visual communications more easily than spoken words. A long stream of verbal orders can be especially challenging. The workplace that ignores this is putting up a barrier.

> I requested written instructions as that is better for my condition but I continued to receive them in a spoken haphazard manner. (Jules, nurse)

Autistic workers may not speak in ways that others easily understand, or may not speak at all.

> I think they [neurotypicals] are just as bad at reading us as we are at reading them: it's just that because they're the majority, their failure to understand us is not as disabling as our failure to understand them. (Lindsay 2012)

Recently, there has been a trend towards 'management speak': a lexicon of buzzwords, from 'vision statement' and 'upskilling' to 'cascading' and 'downsizing'. It is not just autistic workers who find this irritating and opaque.

Autistic workers may struggle to ask for help or information, fearing they will be misunderstood or ridiculed. Mistakes may follow. Alternatively, the autistic worker, keen to get everything absolutely right, may ask no end of questions and be judged as a pain or an idiot.

Where are the rules that say it is OK to ask but not OK to ask too much? Who decided these rules? Is there a specific number of questions that is acceptable? And what do we do if the answer to the question is just as illogical and confusing as the statement we were questioning?

Communication is a form of social interaction and that is where things can get really sticky.

4. SOCIAL INTERACTION

The number one barrier with social interaction at work is that there is so much of it. Charity call-centre worker David (2013) says: 'Talking to 50 people individually a day is disorientating and makes me listless and confused.'

> I practised socialising every night to myself: the right things to say, how to be tactful, how to engage in dialogue. It was a hard process, like programming myself, which most human beings don't do. Sometimes I was accused of being too serious, but I was trying to not be ridiculously eccentric. Practising took up much of my time and alongside the pressures of work, was exhausting. Perfecting my social skills felt like a massive victory for me, but management's response was that I was a nice bloke but not up to standard. (Austin, civil servant)

Next customer please!

Interacting with customers or clients presents particular barriers. Bookshop worker Mark (2014) was criticised by his manager for not maintaining eye contact with shoppers. Not knowing that he was autistic, Mark and his boss were unaware that eye contact can be difficult, even painful, for an autistic person.

Singer Lauren never seemed to last long in previous jobs: 'I do come out with inappropriate things sometimes. When I worked as a shop assistant, I'd sometimes tell people what animal I saw them as! ... Some people didn't like that' (Wheeler 2015b).

Dog groomer Eleanore finds interacting with dogs less distressing than with their owners: 'Dogs are easier; they have special requirements, but they are less fussy.'

Customers can occasionally act in an abusive, even violent, way towards workers, perhaps especially those seen as different or vulnerable.

The barrier has risen higher with the increasing emphasis that 'customer service' places not simply on providing a customer with what he wants but doing it with a smile, an (undefined) appropriate amount of chat, an offer of fries with that and a parting wish for a nice day – policed by a growing army of managers and mystery shoppers.

This is tough for autistic workers and is not what many customers want. They too are neurologically and socially diverse and many are more concerned with the product than with a cheesy grin.

Take one for the team

'Teamwork' seems to be the golden calf of today's workplace: the key to success to which we must all aspire. Its all-pervading presence disables those who do not easily interact or with whom others do not easily interact:

> [A]lthough I had the same to offer employers as other students, I was only ever offered the worst paid and hardest temporary position... This I started to realise was because of my lack of 'teamwork skills' and an inability to socialise with my fellow employees. (Richard 2013)

The barrier rises higher when employers:

- fetishise teamwork: compelling people to work with others more than is actually necessary

- overstate teamwork as a necessary skill

- do not train people (autistic or not) in teamwork skills

- run teams by unwritten rules and neurotypical protocols, leaving autistic team members out of step.

A major teamwork challenge is the meeting, described by Rudy Simone as 'torture...[it] can make us squirm and sweat bullets' (Simone 2010, p.13). Alexandra went to meetings, was unsure what was relevant, tried to remember everything and remembered nothing (Brown 2008, p.48).

Fitting in

Beyond formal teams and meetings, everyday pressure to 'fit in' socially can be just as disabling for autistic workers who do not easily fit. Chatter, 'office politics' and banter may not come naturally to an autistic person.

For some, hearing workmates constantly mocking each other sounds like bullying rather than banter, frightening rather than funny. Others feel that they are there to do a job, not to make 'small talk'.

> No matter how intelligent, capable and kind you are, if everywhere you go people misunderstand and subsequently dislike you, it will have a cumulative impact on your willingness to even try, and will detract from your enthusiasm for your job. (Simone 2010, p.73)

> I joined another team and I wasn't very happy. I found it rather cliquey and felt excluded socially. They went off for a coffee every morning, but didn't invite me to come along and when I did join, they didn't include me in their conversation. (Lauren, civil service scientist)

There is no reason why autistic habits such as avoiding eye or physical contact, unusual postures or facial expressions and 'stimming' behaviours such as rocking, humming or fiddling with objects have to cause a problem at work. But they do: or rather, other people's disdain and discomfort at them does.

Getting by socially at work is hard enough but, for many autistic workers, social events are to be avoided, whether formal or informal:

> I never did any social things with my colleagues outside of work. One girl invited me to a bar for drinks and I was terrified. I could speak to her at work but the idea of

coming up with topics of conversation over drinks was quite horrible. (Jeanette, fast food worker)

On one occasion, we all went to the pub after work, but it was very busy and noisy, one of the group was talking constantly and I couldn't get a word in. I wanted to leave but I couldn't find a way to say I had to go, so I end up just going without saying goodbye. (Josh, data entry assistant)

How does socialising outside work cause problems if it is not even part of the job? It need not, unless:

• the social event is compulsory

• the employer includes staff's (lack of) socialising in appraisal of performance or suitability for promotion

• work decisions are made in the pub.

Many autistic workers get a reputation for being rude or antisocial. Some have prosopagnosis or 'face blindness', an impaired ability to recognise faces, even of people they know well and see often. As a result, they will be judged as rude or odd. Others, myself included, have a notorious autistic bluntness. We do not readily take on protocols about tact or avoiding offence and may even have a compulsion to correct and inform, regardless of, or perhaps unable to anticipate, the impact on others' feelings. Sorry.

I was so stressed with overload I was sometimes a little short when care managers, contracts inspectors etc. came. They had a big meeting about me, which I was not even supposed to know about, let alone attend. I was suicidally depressed at the time and not able to stand up for myself. (Jules, nurse)

Rudy Simone argues that women in particular are expected to be tactful and that autistic women are therefore likely to be judged even more harshly than autistic men (Simone 2010, pp.20–21).

Communication difficulties may make social differences more of a problem than they need be:

Word got back to me that the person I would have been sitting next to had made it clear that she didn't want me sitting next to her. She found me difficult to deal with. That made me feel a bit hurt. A couple of years later, I disclosed [my autism] to this person and she took it really well and said 'Thank you. Now I finally understand why you are the way you are.' Maybe if she had been able to explain to me why she found me difficult, and that I have a tendency to talk on and on, she could have told me to shut up! (Lauren, civil service scientist)

In other cases, an autistic worker's conduct may be more genuinely problematic. This is often the result of distressing working conditions, others' lack of understanding, or never having been told that, or why, particular conduct is not acceptable.

5. SENSORY ISSUES

Autistic people's sensory experiences can be more (or sometimes less) intense than non-autistic people's. So workplaces where the sensory environment is geared to the tolerances of typical people can disable autistic workers. Interior designer Kelly Barker (2015) explains: 'Direct, fluorescent lighting can be problematic for individuals with hyper-sensitivity, as it can distort vision and cause headaches and other issues.' Other factors include sound, light, patterns, smell, computer screens, visual distractions, clothing, ventilation or temperature.

If the background noise from conversations and chatting is affecting me, I feel as though I'm drowning and shutting off, like a computer on the verge of crashing. (Vallantyne 2008, p.146)

If my clothes are too tight, I don't like it, and I can only wear cotton. If I were in a uniformed job, that would be a problem. (Syed, railway track engineer)

My workplace has extensive use of strip lighting, people constantly walking by my desk and too much background noise. (Luke, content writer)

The open-plan office is a particular nightmare:

When I need to concentrate on a task, I want complete silence, which you're never going to get in an open-plan office. When I'm doing a dull task, I quite like to have music on in the background, and again that's something you can't do in an open-plan office. (Keith, journalist)

The office we were in when we started was not good from a sensory point of view. Team members were at opposite ends of the room, it was open plan and noisy. (Josh, data entry assistant)

Sensory difficulties may compound the social ostracism of an autistic worker:

In our delivery office we have a loud speaker radio system that plays music. One morning, Mr X was having sensory issues with the music playing constantly. To eliminate the effects, he tied his gloves over his ears with elastic bands across his head. This resulted in him receiving unwanted attention from the less understanding of the workforce who saw him as an object of fun: 'Look at X', 'Nutty X is at it again.' Mr X ignored these remarks and more worryingly, so did the management. (Paul P., trade union representative)

Stress can also make sensory sensitivity even more intense and uncomfortable. When work pressure was causing her distress, Alexandra (Brown 2008, p.51) notes:

The atmosphere in the building felt stifling and my sense of hearing seemed to become hypersensitive…my ears hurt. The lights seemed to become far too bright, and I found that the only way to make being there more bearable was to walk round with one of my ears covered with my hand.

6. ORGANISING WORK

Executive function is the set of abilities that enables a person to translate motivation into action: to decide to do something and then do it. Autistic people have a range of executive function profiles, which may include unusual features.

An autistic worker may have difficulties with:

- time management

- starting, changing or ending a task

- prioritising

- multitasking.

Some features of the workplace may make these difficulties worse: interruptions, distractions, difficulties or anxieties about particular tasks.

Pace, perfectionism and perseveration

Many workplaces insist that a job is carried out at a predetermined pace or to a schedule:

> I was supposed to do 15 units of work a day, but I was taking a lot of time over each one. I was falling behind and missing targets. It was awful, quite horrendous pressure. Another manager expected me to learn a lot in a short time. It takes me longer to learn than other people, but once I've learned, I can do things perfectly. (Austin, civil servant)

> I think I could take anything that was thrown at me so long as I was in charge of the pace. (Keith, journalist)

Many autistic people prioritise accuracy over speed, to the point of perfectionism. This may produce work of excellent quality but many employers prefer to see the work done promptly and the product sold.

The pressure can cause disabling anxiety. Jeanette (Purkis 2014) had a part-time job washing dishes in a restaurant and was: 'wracked with stress about making a mistake. I didn't think I was just washing dishes. In my mind, it was as if I were a brain surgeon. I got so anxious about the job that I ended up in hospital.'

'Perseveration' refers to repetitive behaviours or difficulty switching tasks and to the tendency to become absorbed in a particular subject to the exclusion of all else, including perhaps the task you are supposed to be doing! This could be quite an asset at work, leading to details and discoveries that improve the process or the product but workplaces usually disapprove of a person deviating from their rigid schemes of work.

Autistic people may find the ways that others work disorderly and frustrating. Nurse Jules says: 'I always, on a matter of principle, left both the office and clinic in perfect condition but I constantly walked into chaos on duty and was expected to clear up after them.'

Work as competition

Where work pits workers against each other, this can be stressful and disabling for autistic (and other) workers. Targets, league tables and performance-related pay all make the production process competitive rather than cooperative. Autistic workers may not fit in to a team very easily but that does not mean that we want to surpass or defeat our workmates.

7. THE TROUBLE WITH MANAGERS

Workers get grief from bosses – that is how the capitalist workplace works – but there are particularly disabling features of management for autistic workers.

Managers may know (or even care) little about autism.

> I told managers [I am autistic] and they said, 'That's terrible', or 'I know a woman who has a son who's got that', but they don't really care. (Keith, journalist)

My boss understands to a certain degree. It's taken a long time to reach this stage and at times he's been exasperated, dismissive and, no doubt unintentionally, made life very hard for me and been totally unable to understand where problems lie or how to solve them. (Neil Shepherd 2008, p.59)

Managers may have their 'blue-eyed boys and girls'.

The manager has an inner circle of people who are always trying to butter-polish him. They are treated with favouritism. But I'm not like that: I keep myself to myself and just get on with my work. (Syed, railway track engineer)

Managers may communicate inappropriately with an autistic employee. David (2013) hates face-to-face coaching from managers: 'I find the situation impossible to read. Their body-language becomes dominating and conflicts with the "I'm just trying to do better" tones of their voices...people doing their best to help me are making me more confused.'

Supervision may be disruptive:

After my diagnosis, [my line manager] started calling me at random times with new instructions. I complained that this was disrupting my schedule and that to suddenly drop things on me by telephone was known to be stressful to autistic people. (Jules, nurse)

While some autistic workers may need hands-on help, others do not. Simone (2010, p.53) says: 'Being trusted vs. being scrutinized impacts a person's confidence and social skills. Trying to relate to customers and coworkers is easier when one is not being watched like a hawk.'

I dislike close supervision. You get supervised by people who have never done a reporter's job but tell reporters how to do our jobs and try to micromanage the process. The old culture of newspapers was that eccentricity was tolerated, you were purely judged by what stories you brought back.

> Now, you need line management agreement to go out and meet somebody! (Keith, journalist)

One barrier is just plain bossiness.

> My manager is a typical, highly-pressured, incompetent middle manager with no real power. He gets a lot dumped on him, and dumps it down. He's totally out of his depth in the job: he's an over-promoted posh boy. (Keith, journalist)

> I represented a member who didn't know he was on the spectrum. He kept getting in trouble at work primarily when people bossed him about and ruined his routines. (Kevin, transport trade union representative)

When assistant scientific officer Richard (2013, p.12) got a new line manager:

> From day one, I could not do anything right… I became a frequent visitor to his office… I did not cope well with this pressure and on at least two occasions damaged doors and lab equipment because of my frustrations. After a protracted period of fighting my impending dismissal (with the help of my union), I left.

The problem is rooted in the power structures of workplaces and of the boss–worker relationship:

> I am not able to control my own destiny. I attribute this solely to the hierarchical nature of this firm, coupled with how this industry is and favouritism towards people who talk as opposed to people who do. (Luke, content writer)

> A care worker, probably exercising that autistic bluntness, challenged a surgeon who left the operating theatre without stopping to wash his hands, and got in trouble when as her 'superior', he took offence. The care worker thought that she was acting correctly, especially as the hospital displayed anti-MRSA posters prominently. (*The Guardian* 2012)

Managing performance

For several of the autistic workers I interviewed, the worst experience was 'performance management', a feature of the modern workplace replete with terminology about aiding improvement but having the opposite effect on many autistic (and other) employees:

> They were always finding an excuse to find a mistake to deem me as below standard. It made me feel like I was being constantly punished. I had to go on an improvement plan, and there was too much of that civil service jargon. The process was awful: first I was put on a warning, I was supposed to appeal, but the correct procedures were not followed and I was sacked. Eventually, my dismissal was reversed and instead I was downgraded. (Austin, civil servant)

> My boss marked me down as 'under-performing' and 'needing improvement'. I disclosed my Asperger's and she made some recommendations but they were never followed through. A new manager put me on a formal improvement plan. My performance had been badly impacted by the environment I was in. She gave me a research project to do but I was left on my own to do it with no-one to turn to for advice. I made a bit of a mess of it. They terminated my contract. (Lauren, civil service scientist)

> I got an oral warning at a local disciplinary; they disciplined me again just two days before that warning expired. I had a breakdown, and was off work for about six months. The doctor referred me to the psychiatrist, and then I got my diagnosis. I went off work because of the way I was being treated here. I could not sleep, I could not eat, I was just going down and down. (Syed, railway track engineer)

Managing attendance

Recent years have seen employers tightening sickness absence policies, usually by issuing warnings to workers who take more than a set number of days off, even when this is for genuine, certificated sickness.

Harsh attendance policies can be especially unfair to autistic and other disabled workers. When oppressive working conditions make an autistic worker unfit to work, the very same workplace adds insult to injury by triggering a disciplinary process. Such policies do not help the worker or even the production process: they merely reinforce who is boss.

The autistic manager?

Managing others may present barriers that make the role unsuitable to some (not all) autistic people: knowing the rules and how flexibly they are supposed to be applied; the 'right' way to speak to people; enforcing rules that seem unfair; the social interaction and stress involved.

> Whenever I took on more management responsibility, I struggled with the increased need to achieve goals through interacting with other people. My lack of emotion and social skills meant that I had to think things through logically and this was not always possible in social situations. (Steve Jarvis 2008, p.111)

An office equipment repair worker with 'legendary expertise' in the subject was promoted to a management position, where he found it hard to cope with the paperwork, corporate policies or egos. He told neither his manager nor his wife that he was struggling. He tried to kill himself (Attwood 2007, p.300).

> My company plans to add management responsibilities to the supervisor's role. The prospect of this is unbearable: I know that I can't discipline people or implement harsh

company policies. I just want to get on with my job as it is now. I don't want to become anyone's boss. (Liza, railway station supervisor)

8. BULLYING, HARASSMENT, DISCRIMINATION

Being ostracised or mocked will usually be hurtful but it may amount to bullying:

> There was constant shouting at me, and belittling, condescending behaviour. I kept having to eat humble pie, because I was afraid that if I spoke out, I would be disciplined for conduct. I'd just count to ten. It was torture. (Austin, civil servant)

The UK Trade Union Congress defines bullying as 'offensive, intimidating, malicious, insulting or humiliating behaviour, abuse of power or authority which attempts to undermine an individual or group of employees and which may cause them to suffer stress.' Harassment and discrimination are defined in Chapter 4.

Autistic workers can be easy targets for bullies, who like to pick on people who are different, whom they perceive as a threat, who lack confidence and/or whom they think others will not defend. Moreover, the autistic worker may not recognise that he is being bullied or may blame himself. Stuart (Vallantyne 2008, pp.148–149) experienced verbal harassment that reduced him to tears: 'A fellow worker told me that the person was picking on me. I didn't think at the time that the person was bullying me. I thought that was part of working life and surviving the workplace.'

Bullies may not even know that their target is autistic: being 'weird', 'annoying' or defiant may be enough. Syed's boss took a dislike to him before either of them knew that he was on the spectrum:

I had got a concession approved by the head of track engineering, but this manager wanted me to change it. I refused, as it had already been approved. From that point onwards, he would instigate disciplinary proceedings for the flimsiest of reasons. He was trying to get me out. He was pushing me through stages so he could dismiss me. I had a breakdown, and was off work for about six months. (Syed, railway track engineer)

Autism-Europe (2014, p.33) reports that autistic workers commonly complain of bullying but that they 'often remark that their concerns are not taken seriously enough by those who are in a position to help them address those concerns.'

Some of the worst cases of mistreatment of autistic workers have seen employers fall foul of the law, including these two from the UK, which were reported by the BBC in 2009 and 2012, respectively:

- Andrew Beck worked as a golf club green keeper and had no problems for 13 years until a new head green keeper arrived. His new boss made him wear highly visible clothing, banned him from using a motorised vehicle, gave him an unfair amount of heavy work, violently knocked a rake out of his hands, pushed him, swore at him, gave him a verbal warning and ridiculed him by giving him a child's game as his staff Christmas present. Andrew resigned, took a claim to the Employment Tribunal for constructive dismissal and disability discrimination, and was awarded £78,000.

- Adam O'Dee has Asperger syndrome and dyslexia and worked as a hotel chef. His boss paid him less than half the minimum wage, and did not pay him for working extra hours. The boss threatened to sack Adam for 'taking too much off the end of a cucumber' and threw frozen bread rolls around the kitchen. Adam resigned, and won an Employment Tribunal claim for unfair dismissal, disability discrimination and breach of minimum wage law, and was awarded £40,000+.

Remember the common view that autistic people lack social skills and empathy? In these two cases at least, it looks more like the boss who is lacking.

Bullying is often the abuse of a position of power. A US survey found that 72 per cent of workplace bullies outranked their target (Healthy Workplace Bill 2015).

Occasionally, an autistic worker may be accused of bullying, perhaps because of the notorious autistic bluntness, perhaps because autistic people do bad things too.

The autistic closet

With so many barriers, many autistic workers, even those who know they are autistic, may keep quiet about it. But the autistic closet may itself present a barrier. Compare these two experiences:

> After I disclosed my Asperger's, my boss recommended that I not be allowed to attend conferences, saying that I wouldn't present a favourable impression to clients. One colleague took my side and said 'If Lauren has something to present, then why send someone else? You wouldn't send someone else on behalf of a black colleague on the assumption that they'd prefer someone who was white.' (Lauren, civil service scientist)

> When I take on an acting job, I tend not to disclose my disability at the audition. Once I get an acting job, however, I disclose my condition almost straightaway. It helps my fellow artistes to understand some of my behaviours such as stimming and talking to myself. This usually, though not always, enables me to avoid misunderstandings and unpleasant situations. (Alain, actor)

9. ALL CHANGE!

Day-to-day disruptions

Predictable routines can help relieve stress from other sources, and unexpected changes can be hard to cope with. Even pleasant surprises may not be entirely pleasant! This does not mean that every autistic worker is completely unable to cope with every unexpected turn of events but it does mean that change or disruption, such as the following examples, may be disabling:

- Some workers have their hours changed at very short notice.

- Mechanical breakdowns can be infuriating: 'A busted fax machine when I was expecting a very important communication was enough to send me into an uncontrollable fit of rage' (Haggarty 2008, p.107).

- 'Work meetings would regularly start late, sometimes hours after the scheduled time. I found it so distressing that by the time the meeting started, I was mentally exhausted and found it difficult to concentrate and keep my temper in the meeting' (Jay, voluntary sector employee).

- 'Hot desking', the recent fad of allocating desks by rotation or task, is definitely inappropriate.

Changes to ways of working

Altering the way in which work is done – hours, processes, office layout – can be a barrier, especially if there is little notice or workers' involvement.

> Following a change in working practices my son could not cope with the increased demands and the conflicting requirements of the role. He became very ill, depressed and stressed, resulting in a breakdown. (Mother of an autistic postal worker)

At the higher end of the Richter scale of workplace change is the grand reorganisation, an earthquake for many workers, especially those on the autistic spectrum. The size of the barrier will depend on the nature and the process of the change.

> Alexandra enjoyed her job in the school library service until the management made radical changes, made staff reapply for their jobs and added extra workload. She became stressed, unhappy, even suicidal. (Brown 2008)

> When the company has one of its reorganisations, it usually accuses the workforce of being afraid of change. But our apprehension comes from bitter experience of past changes. As an autistic person, change will always be a challenge, but I could deal with it much more easily if it were improvements rather than cuts. (Liza, railway station supervisor)

Which leads neatly on to…

10. JOB INSECURITY IN A TIME OF AUSTERITY

Three years into a global economic crisis, Autism-Europe reported that 'amidst the recent budget cuts and austerity measures being implemented in many European countries, people with Autism are suffering significant cuts to the basic services they depend on' (Sullings 2011).

The United Nations (UN) human rights committee that examined the European Union (EU) in August 2015 'expressed its deep concern in relation to this disproportionately adverse and retrogressive effect the austerity measures in the EU [are having] on the lives of persons with disabilities' (European Disability Forum, 2015).

While recent UK legislation demands provision to diagnose autism, shortage of funding has hampered this in practice (Pring 2014). This creates barriers to autistic people getting and keeping a decent job by:

• delaying their access to support services

- preventing them from exercising legal rights such as reasonable adjustments

- driving people to pay for private diagnosis

- causing anxiety and insecurity.

Cuts affect staff as well as clients. Aurélie Baranger, Director of Autism-Europe, told me:

> General insecurity is distressing and I think people with disabilities have been at the forefront of the population affected by unemployment, because if you are going to make redundancies, then you often make people with disabilities redundant first. The current economic climate does not help.

In 2011, a report by the Trade Union Congress found that, in the UK at least, employers had for the first time not disproportionately selected disabled workers for redundancy during the current crisis, although the Trade Union Congress feared that this would change with further public spending cuts. This may be a positive result of legal protections and disability rights campaigns, or the negative result of employers getting rid of disabled workers in other ways. The survey on which this is based does not show specific figures regarding autistic workers.

When employers select workers for redundancy, many of the barriers that the autistic worker had to climb to get the job in the first place arise again. Sophie was made redundant after 21 years working for a local council. On one occasion when it abolished her post, the council assimilated Sophie into a new role but, in a further round of job cutting, it refused to do so and instead required her to take verbal reasoning and written assessments and attend an interview. The employer made some adjustments to the assessments to take account of Sophie's autism but she failed and was dismissed (*Ms S. Henderson v. London Borough of Hackney* [2013] 3203428).

As the job market presents ever higher barriers:

[A]midst all the rhetoric around the purity of good honest toil, it can seem harder than ever to actually find a job today and if you have trouble with, for example, social interaction or organising your time or with painful anxieties, finding, and keeping, a job can actually seem impossible. (Nick 2015)

When unemployment is high, getting a job is more difficult:

They have 100+ applicants for each job so employers have to whittle it down. Maybe they will do that by rejecting people who seem less confident, so autistic people can get knocked back. They don't mean to discriminate, but we can come off worse from the whittling process. (Eleanore, dog groomer)

When staffing levels fall, the remaining workers, including autistic workers, feel the impact:

Because of really tight staffing levels, they can't afford to have too many people not doing the dogsbody stuff at any one time. Doing more with less has become the mantra of the employing class for the last few decades. The physical number of journalists we've got is maybe 20 per cent of what we had in our heyday. The quality of the product has suffered tremendously. (Keith, journalist)

While record numbers of people are in employment, the conditions of that employment are becoming more stressful and insecure. The European Disability Forum (2014) argues that in times of economic crisis, companies reduce the quality of the work environment and that workers agree to compromise or fend for themselves. Employers may maintain profits by not spending money on measures to accommodate autistic staff and by streamlining work processes in conflict with autistic workers' perfectionist drive to create the best product.

A year into the current economic crisis, Labor Notes (US) found that 'union members report increases in verbal abuse, discipline including discharge, crackdowns on attendance, surveillance, hassling to work faster, forced overtime, and a concerted effort to get rid of older workers' (Slaughter 2009). Simone (2010, p.xiv) notes:

Employers and corporations have been going down a certain path for a long time now. With cost-saving techniques being implemented, whether in the form of lay-offs, cramped open-plan offices, energy-efficient fluorescent lights in windowless rooms, or no fully-subsidized health care plan, things are becoming less secure, less pleasant for all.

Employers are using more casualised forms of working, such as contracting out, fixed-term or zero-hours contracts and obtaining staff from agencies. This can cause barriers for autistic workers:

- Trade union representative Kevin told me of an autistic member who was sacked because the hirer company told the contract company that it did not want him on the job. As it was not his own employer's decision to dismiss him, he had no right to challenge it.

- Working on a zero-hours contract or for an agency can involve being told that your working hours (and therefore your income) are only on a weekly, or even daily or hourly basis, with frequent short-notice changes – a nightmare for the autistic person who relies on routine.

- A fixed-term contract causes anxiety about what will happen when its term expires.

Private-sector employers are less accountable than public-sector employers, constrained less by important legislation like the Public Sector Equality Duty (UK). Moreover, a much smaller proportion of private-sector workers than public-sector workers are trade union members – especially in small and medium-sized enterprises – so unions are weaker and less able to defend workers' rights and improve conditions in those workplaces.

Some autistic adults, denied the opportunity of paid employment, resort to unpaid voluntary work instead. This may be useful experience and enjoyable, but it is exploitation:

> Michael worked for a while as a volunteer with arts with more severely autistic young people. He really liked it. It would have suited him well if that had been a paid, permanent post at a properly funded project, but it isn't. (Kate, Michael's sister)

> I started work as a volunteer at a gallery that I liked visiting. The paid staff loved having me there as I was very enthusiastic and they didn't have to pay me. (Purkis 2014)

After repeatedly parting company with paid jobs when she experienced panic attacks, Cathy (2015) now does voluntary work, saying that 'it is a much more understanding environment and I can decide not to go if I am feeling anxious'.

If such work is valuable, why is it not paid? And why does paid work not provide an understanding environment and allow you to stay away when you feel anxious?

There is a common view that excuses insecure employment on the grounds that people can no longer expect a 'job for life'. In my 2013 book, *Plundering London Underground*, train driver 'Jock' (the late Brian Munro) delivered this riposte:

> Why can't people have a job for life? Why do people have to have an expectation that they can be thrown on the dole for whatever reason? To say that the workers in Britain should be in constant anxiety and fear of unemployment or constant anxiety about their ability to raise their children, pay their bills, pay their mortgage is wrong. It should be a positive thing to have a job for life. (Booth 2013, p.77)

Is self-employment or freelance work a viable alternative?

> I worked freelance and did OK, but it's never reliable: it can be a famine or a feast. Many of the things that people say they hate about it, like being on your own all the time

and working from home, I loved. You don't have one boss, you have control over your working day. You can control the pace. On the other hand, there's no sick pay, no paid holiday. (Keith, journalist)

It is hard to find a steady stream of income as a professional artist at any time, and having Asperger's Syndrome can add to these difficulties. Many artists do other types of work to support themselves when their art is not making money for them, and it is this that we struggle with. Although I take care to avoid landing in debt, the current economic climate means that the bottom can fall out from under you very quickly. My condition and financial situation have given me a lot of stress. (Alain, actor)

Michael is an artist. The JobCentre offered him help to set up a small business, but they haven't got any money to give or any real expertise. He went for the idea at one point, but it didn't work: it's very competitive, it's not realistic. He was told some things he could have done to make it work: approaching cafés and asking them to put his work on the wall, setting up a website, giving himself a brand. But you have to push yourself forward, you have to initiate social interaction, and he finds that very difficult. (Kate, Michael's sister)

I worked out that to do my dream of singing, I'd be self-employed. This seemed like a good option. I felt that being a singer would mean there would be more room for quirkiness and creativity, so I would be able to keep the job for longer. (Lauren Lovejoy, in Wheeler 2015b)

Chapter 3

Remove those Barriers!

1. GETTING WORK
Starting behind the starting line

To give autistic job applicants a fair start with others we need an education system that fulfils the potential of all, whatever their neurological status, and an employment system that does the same. The former is beyond the scope of this book; the latter is its mission.

Until we achieve these transformations, autistic people's employment chances can improve if employers:

- avoid insisting on qualifications or employment history not essential for the job

- provide training to fill gaps left by inadequate education and prior employment

- waive or reduce requirements for people whose qualifications or job history do not reflect their true abilities

- use other means to assess an applicant's suitability.

Get a job!

Where the barrier is lack of support in getting a job, remove it by providing support.

The UK's National Institute for Health and Clinical Excellence (2012) recommends individual supported employment programmes for autistic adults with mild or no learning disability. Autism-Europe (2014, p.x) recommends assessing autistic people to establish what jobs may be suitable.

> When I left college I was placed in the available jobs rather than those which capitalized on my strengths... In retrospect on leaving college I should have been assessed properly instead of being sent to the available jobs which were inevitably inappropriate for my abilities. (Emma Beard, local authority worker 2008, p.166)

Government assistance does exist but it will only help a few people unless it becomes more widely available, more reliably funded and equipped with a proper understanding of autism.

The UK's JobCentre Plus has Disability Employment Advisers but there are not enough of them sufficiently knowledgeable about autism (National Autistic Society 2011, p.11).

Access to Work (AtW) funds equipment and support to help disabled people overcome work-related obstacles. It would help more autistic jobseekers if it had a higher budget than the £108m it spent in 2013/14. The National Autistic Society (2013) contends that the potential benefits of increasing AtW funds will not be realised unless assessors understand autism properly and autistic people are made aware of their rights to access it.

> My job coach is provided by JobCentre Plus, and is helping me find a job. My coach is very understanding. With AS [Asperger's Syndrome] Mentoring, you have a first meeting, a free consultation, then you pay per hour. Mine is paid for by the Access To Work fund. My mum and I had to find AS Mentoring and tell JobCentrePlus about it. I wasn't just given the support that I need: I had to go and find some of it myself. (Eleanore, dog groomer)

In the US, there are Vocational Rehabilitation (VR) services for qualified disabled people but where VR agencies cannot fund all applicants they may implement 'order of selection' (a federal government requirement to prioritise individuals with higher needs) and autistic people, especially those with strong intellectual abilities, may lose out (Lesco 2011).

The Australian government gives examples of support that can be offered to autistic jobseekers and workers on its JobAccess website (Australian Government 2015). It has an Employee Assistance Fund that provides work assessments to identify modifications. However, Autism Asperger's Advocacy Australia (Buckley 2015) argues that 'There is little prospect that existing programs and plans will improve employment outcomes for people with ASD... The pathways into employment services... are essentially non-existent for many people with ASD.'

A parliamentary question in the UK House of Lords observed:

> WorkChoice, the scheme intended to help the disabled into employment, has had very little success in helping people with autism to find a job, while the Work Programme itself seems to find great difficulty in placing anyone with autism in employment at all. (House of Lords Hansard 2012)

Autistic people can only apply for jobs they know about: advertised publicly, published in suitable formats and circulated to employment support services as well as JobCentres and newspapers.

Job adverts and job descriptions can minimise barriers to autistic applicants by:

- being clear and concise, using straightforward language
- avoiding jargon and unnecessary information
- including information about support, adjustments and the workplace environment

- including only job requirements that are objectively necessary

- avoiding specifying personality types required, such as 'outgoing' or 'team player'; instead specifying job roles such as 'serving customers'.

Job application forms can minimise barriers similarly: straightforward, no jargon or unnecessary questions, the option of submitting the application online or on hard copy and space to request further information or adjustments.

Interviews and other methods

Some books provide advice to autistic applicants on how to behave in interviews. They can be useful but this book advocates changing the interview. When Bissonnette (2013b, p.131) argues that 'Companies do not want to hire individuals who are perceived as unfriendly, arrogant, unenthusiastic, poor listeners, resistant to the ideas of others, or just difficult', this writer advises that they consider adjusting their perceptions.

Autistic applicants will benefit from the opportunity to prepare for the interview, including:

- adequate notice, by post and/or email

- specified start and end times

- information about the venue, how to get there, accessibility and the sensory environment

- details of the interview's format, who will be there and any tests involved

- the interview questions

- practice papers for tests

- details of what to bring and any dress code

- a statement of commitment to equalities and accessibility

- information on how to ask questions and request adjustments.

The benefits of these measures will be lost if the interview does not follow the format notified in advance: for example, if it starts late, if requests for adjustments are ignored or if test questions are printed in a different format from the practice papers.

Robert's employer sent him practice papers for his promotion assessment but when he sat the tests, he found that they were in a different format. This disorientated him and he failed. The company did not seem to realise that this was a problem as other, non-autistic, applicants adjusted to the difference.

In the interview itself, autistic people will be better able to describe their suitability for the job if they are allowed to:

- bring a support worker or other companion:

  > They allowed my NAS support worker to attend the interview with me, which made me feel less nervous. She explained Asperger's to the interviewers and emphasised that I have strengths as well as weaknesses. As there were two interviewers, it felt more even having two people on my side as well! (Josh, data entry assistant)

- take time to acclimatise to the room before the interview starts

- take time to process questions and formulate answers

- give a presentation or show examples of previous work rather than just answer questions

- be judged on ability to do the job, not on irrelevant social factors such as eye contact, rocking on their chair or playing squash at the weekend.

It will also be helpful if questions are:

- straightforward, concise, direct, relevant, jargon free
- concrete not hypothetical (e.g. 'Tell me about an occasion when equipment you were using stopped working: what did you do?' rather than 'What would you do if your equipment stopped working?')
- closed not open (e.g. 'What were your duties in your last job?' rather than 'Tell me about your last job').

Similarly, written assessments can be made more accessible to autistic applicants, with:

- a separate room to sit the tests, with low sensory stimuli
- extra time to complete the test
- questions in straightforward language
- graphic rather than text-only questions.

Stress interviews and psychometric/personality tests are inaccurate at best, abusive and discriminatory at worst. There is no place for them in a fair recruitment process.

Practical tests will usually provide a fairer means of assessing an autistic applicant.

> We argue for employers to allow autistic applicants to carry out a specific, concrete task to show what they can do rather than be judged on social behaviour like small talk in an interview. (Aurélie Baranger, Autism-Europe)

Pacelli (2014, p.52) argues: 'An autistic person can often most effectively show his skills through a sample activity, such as proofing a sample document for an editing position.'

Actors audition for roles, rather than attend interviews or sit exams about how good they would be in the part. Why not apply this principle to other jobs? Practical assessments are recommended by, amongst others, the UK government

(Department for Work and Pensions and National Autistic Society 2012, p.9).

The ideas in this section can also apply to promotion, redeployment, even selection for redundancy. Additional helpful measures may be possible for an existing employee going through these processes – for example, holding interviews or tests in familiar venues.

Trade unions have long demanded objective rather than subjective criteria for processes such as these: definite measures of selecting the person rather than managers picking people they like or who have flattered them. The latter is unfair in many ways, including to autistic workers: the socially awkward person is less likely to be the boss's favourite.

The proposals in this section would not unfairly disadvantage non-autistic workers. Most would benefit them. So why not post clearly worded job adverts, scrap psychometric testing and replace interviews with practical assessments for everyone?

2. GETTING ON WITH THE JOB

It will be easier for an autistic person to get on with a new job if the employer:

- provides key information before the first day, covering issues such as working hours, breaks, leave, dress code, facilities, transport

- helps the workplace's trade union to provide the new recruit with information about the benefits of membership and who to contact

- organises an induction programme, including orientation around the workplace, meeting key colleagues and clear information about the working day and work processes:

> The preparation for my job was good: there was lots of training. Instructions and information are given

clearly, although at one point I was given a huge manual on how the data system worked which was rather intimidating. (Josh, data entry assistant)

- asks workers what their preferences are for communication, sensory environment, and so forth; this could be via a questionnaire given to all employees.

Barriers to training can be reduced by taking account of the different learning styles of autistic people. Moreover, autistic learners will benefit from one-to-one training and from learning about aspects of work that are often assumed and therefore not taught: for example, meeting skills or time management.

An effective induction and training programme will help to build confidence and identify the autistic worker's strengths.

It may also identify some aspects of a job that suit a person more than others. For example, a worker might excel at the core, technical part of the job while the customer interaction part might cause problems. Tony (2013) states: 'I'm better equipped for "back office" tasks than "front office" ones so I've become more selective in what I'm prepared to do.' Remove the barrier that this presents by rearranging duties among the workforce. If an autistic person is a skilled car mechanic, does that person really have to deal with motorists booking in and picking up their cars? Or could she do the mechanical work while others who prefer social interaction deal with the customers?

If it is not possible to reallocate work, barriers can be reduced by providing extra support for the more challenging role, such as supplementary training, mentoring or visual prompts.

It is not just autistic workers who can benefit from training to overcome barriers faced by autistic workers. Training for managers and workers generally can help by:

- educating them about autism and neurological diversity

- teaching them how to communicate directly and effectively

- introducing autism-friendly working practices

- reducing harassment and bullying.

Many sources advise employers to provide training to managers and staff about autism when there is an identified autistic worker in their workplace (e.g. Department for Work and Pensions and National Autistic Society 2012, p.11) but why wait for this? If training and awareness about autism were standard in workplaces, rather than implemented only when an identified autistic worker arrives, this would:

- prevent embarrassingly counterproductive experiences like Lauren's:

  > I only told my manager and my personal buddy about my autism, but they decided to give the whole team Asperger Awareness Training with me out of the room. Maybe they did it so they could talk openly about what they thought of me. I heard from the job coach that they took it rather badly, and they became more hostile towards me: 'So that's her excuse is it?' The job coach told me that it was my boss who insisted on me being out of the room, and she now admits that it was a mistake to have gone along with his demands. (Lauren, civil service scientist)

- take the focus away from individuals, making them less self-conscious and less of a target

- help to normalise the presence of autistic people in the workplace

- reduce barriers facing workers who do not know they are autistic, have not been diagnosed, or who do not wish to disclose their autism.

Guidance from the National Institute for Health and Clinical Excellence (2012, 9.3.1.11/12) recommends that employment support continue after the job starts. Luke Beardon, a lecturer in autism, argues that 'an employer...should not automatically expect the individual to know what support structures need to be put in place' (Edmonds and Beardon 2008, p.109). Our society's understanding of autism is so limited that even autistic people may not be aware of the exact assistance we need or what we can demand. Support from an advocate – an autism support worker and/or a trade union representative – can make a significant and positive difference.

Autism-Europe (2014, pp.40–41) reports that supported approaches to employment for autistic people 'have proved very effective in assisting them to gain and maintain jobs that are appropriate to their skills and abilities', particularly if the support is specialised to address their particular needs. The National Autistic Society (UK) found that 63 per cent of autistic adults who received specialised support gained jobs suitable to their abilities and education compared with only 25 per cent of those who received general, non-specialised support. If the employer runs an occupational health service, autism training for all its staff, and/or appointment of staff who have specialised in autism, will make it better able to provide support for autistic workers.

An employment support worker or job coach provided to an individual autistic worker can help by:

- educating the employer
- acting as an intermediary between the worker and the employer
- identifying a mentor at work
- providing practical and emotional support
- 'troubleshooting'
- identifying additional support or adjustments.

SHELTERED WORKSHOPS?

The term 'sheltered workshop' refers to a workplace where disabled people are employed separately from others. However, these institutions have attracted criticism, including that:

- they segregate autistic people

- wages are low and rights limited

- jobs are often below the employees' skill levels

- autistic people may have had little say in the decision that they would work there

- the organisations that run them 'profit substantially from exploiting their labour and offer them little or no opportunity to develop their skills for the open market' (Autism-Europe 2014, p.42).

Acknowledging these criticisms, Autism-Europe argues (2014, pp.44–46) that sheltered workshops are the best option for some autistic people with high support needs. It offers an example of good practice: TERLAB, a not-for-profit body in Barcelona, which employs 42 autistic adults.

For an accurate assessment of initiatives such as this, we need to hear the experience and opinions of autistic workers themselves.

Those autistic people who are genuinely more suited to a 'sheltered workshop' environment will enjoy better support, wages and rights if these organisations are not run for profit but are publicly owned and accountable, governed with the involvement of autistic workers and their trade unions.

SUPPORTED EMPLOYMENT AND SELF-DETERMINED STRUCTURES

Unlike sheltered workshops, the various forms of supported employment involve paid work in an integrated work setting with ongoing support. They include placement in a mainstream workplace, autism-specific workgroups and integration into small businesses.

Autism-Europe (2014, pp.36–41) cites studies showing that supported employment delivers better outcomes than sheltered workshops, in terms of pay, social integration, job satisfaction and self-esteem. It gives several examples.

Government publications from the UK also cite examples, usually very positively (e.g. Department for Work and Pensions and National Autistic Society 2012). However, some autistic workers' experience may not live up to the brochures' claims.

> I did six months at a company that the National Autistic Society has a special relationship with, as part of their autistic work placement programme. A workplace health adviser assessed me and recommended regular meetings, but I hardly saw my manager at all during the first month. I was given some work, but never enough to fill my day. It made me feel like a charity case, that I was just there to salve their conscience and allow them to tick a box. Towards the end of my placement, I did have some meetings and expressed my frustrations, and the boss asked me to give a presentation on how to improve the workplace for autistic people. (Lauren)

There are also several examples of autistic workers forming cooperatives:

- Laboratoria di Esplorazione Multimedial is an Italian web and graphic design and translation service set up by people with Asperger Syndrome who met online (Autism-Europe 2014, p.48).

- Passwerk, launched in Amsterdam in 2008, provides information technology services, including maintaining the station gates on the Brussels metro:

  > Passwerk adjusts as an employer to meet their abilities, strengths and competencies, offering a well-adapted workplace...Where the limitations associated with an employee's autism preclude them from being able to carry out a given task, then other employees

> contribute. Passwerk employs 'job coaches' who step in at such times and work closely with the employees who have autism. There is one job coach for every seven employees. (Autism-Europe 2011)
>
> A genuine assessment of workers' effectiveness will take into account their experiences.

3. COMMUNICATION

We have explained autism as a neurological variant: atypical brain wiring. In computer terminology, perhaps it is like comparing iOS to neurotypicality's Windows. In their early days, iOS and Windows could not communicate with each other but now they can. Protocols and systems developed that enabled them to understand each other. Similarly, we can bridge the communication gap between autistic and non-autistic people.

Most workplaces have communication processes that assume neurotypicality, thus putting up barriers against those who do not fit. How can those barriers be removed or reduced?

A workplace will be more autism friendly if communication is:

- straightforward: free from, for example, jargon, ambiguity, sarcasm, idioms, abstraction and exaggeration

- manageable: in chunks rather than overwhelming quantities

- flexible: avoiding a narrow workplace 'dialect' spoken only by insiders

- not context dependant: not relying on vocal emphasis, tone or volume, facial expression, hand gestures, body language, eye contact, nods or winks

- comprehensive: without leaving information or expectations unstated.

None of this implies 'dumbing down' or speaking slowly and loudly in that excruciatingly patronising way that some people do to those they consider stupid. Clarity is important not because autistic workers are less intelligent but because autistic and neurotypical people process differently. Clarity reduces misunderstanding.

An autism-friendly workplace would allow a variety of communication formats. In countries or workplaces where more than one language is spoken (e.g. Wales, Canada, airports), signs, announcements and other communications are multilingual. Communication can be multineurological too, by:

- providing information and instructions in written and visual formats and by demonstration, as well as verbally

- using calendars, videos, slideshows and other media

- using handouts with information such as workplace vocabulary and terminology

- allowing workers adequate time to process information.

Crucially, an autism-friendly workplace would ask for and facilitate each worker's preferred means of communication.

Civil servant P. J. Hughes (2008, p.37) was allowed to use emails and letters as his main communication forms, rather than the telephone (many autistic people do not like using the phone).

People may understand communication better if they record it in their preferred way: repeating it, making notes, doodles, visual reminders and so forth.

Autistic people who do not speak at all can still communicate. There are plenty of jobs that do not actually require the post holder to speak.

It will be easier to ask questions if they are positively welcomed and are not answered with 'that's easy/obvious', 'common sense should tell you', 'you know what I mean', or 'go figure'.

Communication skills training will help both autistic and non-autistic workers. Training or coaching can teach an autistic person to recognise non-verbal signals; it can also help a non-autistic person to rely less on these signals.

4. SOCIAL INTERACTION

Tony Attwood (2007, p.298) recommends support and guidance for autistic workers in areas such as interpersonal skills and personal hygiene. There are significant benefits to autistic workers from support in these areas. Just as a workplace would teach new staff the technical vocabulary of a job, why not also teach them the social vocabulary?

Non-autistic workers and managers can benefit from social-skills training too. Although it is a common view that autistic people lack social skills, it is important to remember that:

- We do not have a monopoly on this.

- What constitutes 'social skills' tends to be determined by the dominant group. (Who says that it is OK to talk obsessively about football but not about railway timetables?)

- Offering training only to autistic workers misses out those who are undiagnosed or unwilling to reveal their autism.

- Training only autistic workers reinforces the (inaccurate, prejudiced) view that only they lack social skills:

    Learning about social skills benefits us all. Coworkers can learn to be patient and make an effort to give autistic employees some leeway in social skills that might be lacking. In an ideal workplace, everyone would be treated this way, regardless of whether or not a disability is known. (Pacelli 2014, p.113)

Social interaction among a diverse population, such as a workforce, is a process of negotiation. A democratic, collective discussion to agree any etiquette or social protocols is likely to be much more effective than leaving the rules unwritten or imposing them from on high. The workplace can also reduce the demands it makes for social interaction through:

- regular breaks

- the facility to work alone for at least some of the time:

> My boss and the people I work with know I cannot handle a lot of social interaction so they do not pressure me too much and leave me alone to work quietly on my own. I have a room where I can work alone. They know I am happiest like this, and they are very happy and pleased with all the work I do. (Jacqueline 2013, hospital administration worker)

- a workstation away from others, either in a separate room or at the edge of a larger area and away from social areas such as canteens or the coffee machine:

> I would have exclusion zones around desks so that autistic employees are less prone to suffering from sensory overload. (Luke, content writer)

- trying to ensure that social interaction is prearranged, predictable, in a familiar place and in a preferred communication format

- allowing staff the option to work from home whilst ensuring they are not coerced into doing so and that it does not become a pretext for isolating them or withdrawing support

> By homeworking, I have grabbed back a whole layer of control over the work process. I can get closer to doing the job the way I know it should be done. And

it enables you to integrate work and life a bit. (Keith, journalist)

My GP recommended that I be allowed to work from home, but management refused. The reason they gave was that my performance was not good. They treat working from home as a reward for good performance, when it should be a reasonable adjustment. (Syed, railway track engineer)

Next customer please!

The barriers created by interaction with clients or customers can be reduced by:

- reallocating duties among workers, with their agreement:

    It would suit me better if someone else was doing the client interaction and I am just working with the dog. (Eleanore, dog groomer)

- training

- providing scripts for various situations

- regular breaks from customer contact

- prioritising doing the job in a polite and practical way rather than, for example, eye contact, smiles, handshakes

- educating customers and clients

- making it clear that abuse of staff will not be tolerated

- removing any element of appraisal, especially of pay, based on subjective 'customer satisfaction'.

Teams and meetings

Let's look at reducing three particular teamwork barriers in Chapter 2:

- Don't fetishise teamwork. An objective assessment of the job can establish the degree of teamwork actually needed, so that no-one is forced to do more of it than necessary.

- If there is a lack of training, provide it. Teamwork training can teach an autistic worker the skills required in conversation, for example; it can also teach non-autistic staff to communicate clearly and to accept autistic mannerisms and differences. Training can be followed up with individual coaching, both for autistic workers and for any neurotypical worker who is struggling to relate to an autistic colleague.

- If there are unwritten rules and neurotypical protocols, agree and write the rules to suit everyone. A collective process of agreeing how the team will work together can enable each person to contribute in the most effective way.

Consider whether the autistic worker needs to attend meetings, if she would prefer not to:

OK, so your Aspergic employee doesn't like going to team meetings – what about if they get the salient points of the meeting sent to them in an email? They still get the same information as everyone but don't have to be put through a nightmare situation. A simple workaround. (Shepherd 2008, p.65)

Meetings can be made easier for those who do attend by:

- sending the agenda and other relevant information in advance

- allowing participants to submit contributions in writing or as a presentation

- starting and finishing the meeting on time

- running the meeting in a friendly but formal way: introducing speakers; firm and fair chairing; ensuring only one person speaks at a time; avoiding or explaining jargon.

Training and/or coaching in meeting skills may also help, although it is important that this is aimed at everyone, not just at making autistic workers conform to neurotypical protocols. Employment coach Barbara Bissonnette (2013a, p.33) reports that her client, Adam, stared at his notepad during staff meetings while listening intently to everything said. His supervisor wrongly inferred that he was not paying attention and the coach advised Adam to look at people when they spoke. His supervisor was pleased when he did. But Bissonnette's report offers no evidence that Adam was actually paying more attention in the meetings: with the effort of making eye contact, he may even have been less attentive. Why not coach the supervisor to accept that different people behave differently when concentrating? Or coach both Adam and his supervisor? Better still, coach everyone.

Fitting in

The number one strategy for removing barriers to 'fitting in' is to accept us for who we are. Autistic flautist Steve Barker told the *Independent* (2012) that if society wants autistic people to participate, then it has to let us be ourselves, not just when it is convenient, but in all areas of our lives. Steve feels that he is accepted when he is performing on stage, but that society creates difficulties for him when he is off stage. He asks that society accepts autistic people with all our characteristics, just as it does typical people.

If a worker 'fits in' with her current workmates, then leave well alone! Alexandra Brown (2008, p.53) 'would like to stay where I am if at all possible, because people seem generally accepting of some of my ways, like skipping and galloping along the corridors at right angles, and some of the things I say'.

Managers and colleagues may need to be trained to accept differences and eccentricities. It is certainly preferable to educate people to accept that some autistic people walk on their toes than to tell autistic workers to stop doing it or allow others to mock, bully or avoid them.

> When I told my boss that I had been diagnosed as autistic, he agreed to let me go on a training course but refused my request to have a basic leaflet about autism available to my workmates. It felt like he thought that I needed to learn how to deal with autism but no-one else did! (Jay, voluntary sector employee)

In most jobs, some social interaction is necessary but pressuring an autistic worker to socialise beyond that may cause distress. We can remove some of the barriers by taking the following steps:

- social events to be optional
- socialising not to be included in staff appraisal
- no work decisions to be made on social occasions.

The barrier of autistic bluntness can be addressed through training and raising awareness (for the whole workforce). I constantly pick faults in systems, policies and ways of doing things. I know that it rubs some people up the wrong way (although others welcome the criticisms being articulated). I do not want to stop doing it altogether, as my points may be valid and improvements may result, but I would like to learn to do it only over important things and without hurting people's feelings. I would like people to accept that I can put those views forward without getting defensive and personal about it.

Criticisms and disagreements can often be more effectively (and tactfully) dealt with through agreed procedures rather than leaving them to the volatile terrain of personal interaction. Under collective bargaining, the trade union represents the collective views of workers and tables to the employer demands for improved working conditions and objections to proposed changes that it considers detrimental. Channelling ideas and criticisms through collective bargaining amplifies the workers' voice in workplace matters and removes the personal 'sting' from raising criticism.

Beyond simple bluntness, though, there can be genuinely problematic conduct by autistic workers. In Chapter 2 we identified three particular triggers and each trigger suggests action that might help:

- If there are *distressing working conditions,* make them less distressing, implementing measures suggested in this book and elsewhere; provide support to deal with distress and anger.

- If there is a *lack of understanding* from others, educate the workforce.

- Sometimes *employees have never been told that conduct is unacceptable* – to prevent this, provide training, clear codes and rules; there should be collective decision making by the workforce about what is and is not OK.

SPACE TO DE-STRESS

If workplaces were more autism friendly, autistic workers would experience less stress and anxiety. But the wider world remains stressful and anxiety remains a constant presence. So autistic workers will benefit from strategies and space to de-stress.

Work out a strategy to alleviate stress:

- Allow the autistic worker himself to determine the strategy, with support where required. Luke Beardon argues that finding out what an individual needs to do to relax and providing the opportunity to do so 'can make a huge difference in the fight between meaningful employment and the benefits office' (Edmonds and Beardon 2008 p.17).

- Perhaps involve a nominated contact person. P. J. Hughes (2008, p.37) says: 'When I need to stress out or want to have a chat or whatever, I have a telephone number to ring.'

- Provide techniques and therapies for relaxation and to manage anxiety.

- Provide reassurance that minor matters such as occasional lateness will not have severe consequences.

- Avoid the stressful atmosphere created by harsh disciplinary and attendance policies and shouty managers.

- Provide regular breaks. Schedule these during the working day and allow extra breaks when the need arises, such as after a difficult interaction with a customer.

- Facilitate a specific, chosen activity during breaks.

All workers can suffer from stress, and neurotypical workers have anxiety management strategies too. They may drink coffee, chat with colleagues, smoke, or phone a friend. Autistic ways of relaxing are often seen as socially unacceptable. Remove that barrier by accepting and facilitating everyone's preferred coping mechanism. There is no good reason for skipping round the car park to be any less tolerated than chatting at the water cooler.

De-stressing will be helped by the provision of dedicated relaxation spaces. One worker may benefit from lying down in a quiet, dark room; another from her preferred form of stimming, perhaps rocking or spinning; another may need to be loud and vocal. If she does this within sight or hearing of others, the autism-friendly workplace will accept this. If she prefers to do this in privacy, it will provide an appropriate room or space that she can access alone. A communal, open-access staff room is not enough.

Some autistic adults have spoken about 'burnout', described on the Planet Autism blog as 'resulting from the attempts to "be normal", fit in and keep up. It can creep up on you, it can hit you any time'. Recovery can take some time, so it would be helpful for workplaces to have a disability leave or career break policy that allows for the autistic worker to take enough time away, with the job still there to return to.

5. SENSORY ISSUES

'Universal Design' is a concept incorporated in the United Nations Convention on the Rights of Persons with Disabilities. It has been described as 'the design of products, environments, programmes and services to be usable by all people, to the greatest extent possible, without the need for adaptation or specialized design'. Sara Gardner of Autism Spectrum Navigators explains that Universal Design 'makes workplaces comfortable and accommodating for those with autism as well as those with other disabilities, while not infringing on employees without disabilities' (Pacelli 2014, p.62).

Dr Magna Mostafa, a 'world-leading expert on designing built environments for autism' suggests allocating spaces in a logical order and with clear functions and argues that the sensory environment is 'central to the process of autism-friendly design' (Mostafa 2015). Voluntary sector worker Paul says: 'Reducing sensory stimulus, or facilitating autistic people to work away from it, will help.'

As different people on the autistic spectrum have different sensitivities, many effective measures involve giving control to each worker over their sensory environment, for example allowing sensory breaks and/or allocating a workspace away from the stimulus that aggravates or distracts her.

Our new office is much better. My team is all together and it's less noisy. I sit by the window so I can control the temperature and light, using the blinds when necessary. They took my needs into account. I sit at a desk in the corner and listen to music through headphones so I don't get distracted by noise. (Josh, data antry assistant)

Offering these choices to all staff will ensure that any sensitivities of non-autistic people are also addressed. Where someone does need specific measures, an autism-aware workforce is less likely to complain about or mock that workmate. Administrative worker Kay Ribbons asked for a purple filter to reduce sensory overload from her computer screen, but colleagues accused her of 'milking it', using her autism to get special treatment. Ribbons, who is now unemployed, said that the problem was ignorance. Her colleagues genuinely believed that she was singling herself out to get something extra, but she actually needed the equipment to do her job properly (*The Guardian* 2012).

Here are some suggestions to alleviate sensory overstimulation or distraction:

- Light and other visual stimuli:

  - Avoid fluorescent lights; use natural or full-spectrum light instead.

  - Provide dimmer switches on lights.

  - Provide individual desk lights.

  - Provide diffusers over light sources.

  - Mute bright colours.

  - Reduce overbearing décor and cluttered walls; keep notices to noticecases.

  - Apply Display Screen Equipment regulations and good practice.

  - Provide coloured overlays and filters to help visual processing.

- Sound:

  - Provide earplugs.

- Provide noise-cancelling headphones.
- Provide white-noise machines or software.
- Provide a quieter workspace, cubicle, or partitioned area.
- Provide therapies and techniques to develop tolerance of triggering sounds.
- Food and other smells:
  - Shield workspaces from smells from machinery, pungent substances and emissions, food preparation and eating areas.
  - Allow workers to eat away from the main communal eating area if they wish.

There is evidence linking autism with digestive problems and some autistic people follow specific diets. A workplace canteen or vending machine stocking a range of food, including vegetarian and gluten-/dairy-free and organic options, will enable these workers and others with speciality diets to participate in workplace eating provision.

- Fabrics and touch:
  - Avoid upholstery that is overly complex or patterned.
  - Apply dress codes and uniform only when necessary and as flexibly as possible; prioritise comfort over conformity.
  - State clearly any dress code or requirement.
  - Allow workers to choose fabrics to avoid those that cause distress and pain.
  - Avoid extremes of temperature and allow individual control over temperature; this will help workers who are hypersensitive to heat or cold.

6. ORGANISING WORK

Autism-Europe (2014, p.29) argues: 'A high degree of structure, predictability and routine can help the person with autism perform in the position, though this does not necessarily mean that the job should be tedious or boring.' Changes to job structure, the working day, etc. can remove barriers to autistic people:

- Minimising interruptions:

  > Our pharmacist suggested I had a 'do not disturb' tabard for the hectic morning medication round to minimise mistakes, but the owner would not allow it. (Jules, nurse)

- Provide assistance with scheduling and prioritisation, breaking larger tasks into smaller chunks.

- Allow workers to have collective control over the production process, and individual workers to have control over their individual roles as far as practical. Where this cannot (or does not) happen, give precise information about expectations and how work is done.

- Make provision for preferred activities during breaks.

- Provide suitable working hours: for example, reduced hours, at least at first; better still, shorter working hours for the whole workforce (without loss of pay).

- Allow workers to be able to start and finish earlier or later than others:

  > Personally, I hate arriving at work and walking into a busy, crowded office. I like to commence work early in the morning, as it is nice to be the first to arrive in the office at 7.30 a.m. as it means that I can work in peace and without distraction for a while! (Haggarty 2008, p.106)

> They have allowed me to come in at different hours. I come in at 11 o'clock and work late. My job does not require me to work in a particular office or at particular times. (Syed, railway track engineer)

- Make hours predictable: for example, give maximum possible notice of changes of duty times; set a guaranteed number of hours per week; ensure a set of rules is agreed between the union and the employer governing the number of days and hours worked, rest periods and time between duties:

> We call it the Framework Agreement. It restricts how much management can mess us about and means that we have a reasonable idea of what we are doing from week to week. It's not perfect, but we try to defend and strengthen it while the company repeatedly tries to dilute it! (Liza, railway station supervisor)

There are practical tools that can help with organising work. Tools chosen and customised by autistic workers themselves will be most effective, such as:

- a personal workstation
- checklists, labels, notebooks, wallcharts
- apps and electronic organisers
- a staff directory with names and photos; name markers on doors or cubicles.

A mentor can be useful by:

- helping with transport to and from work
- explaining and reminding about work tasks
- 'translating' communications
- recognising anxiety triggers and acting to reduce them

- educating others and challenging intolerant or problematic behaviour by colleagues.

As well as acting as a companion and advocate, a trade union representative can collectivise individual issues: extrapolating from one (autistic) union member's experiences and needs to put forward demands that will improve the workplace for all.

Pace, perfectionism, perseveration

Liberate those autistic strengths and talents by removing barriers and straitjackets that profit-driven business so typically builds around creative work:

- Find scope within a production process to enable new ideas and productive tangents to be explored and staff to go at their own pace where possible.

- Employ enough staff instead of the bare minimum:

  Hire enough people to do the job. Don't leave us understaffed and screaming for resources and then moaning because the competition gets more good stories! With enough staff, there would be less stress. People would be so much more productive: you could actually think straight rather than fight fires the whole time. (Keith, journalist)

- A mentor can help to spot when pace, perfectionism and/ or perseveration may become a problem and help autistic workers in ways they feel comfortable with.

Valuing autistic workers' abilities is essential but beware of this becoming a pretext for exploitation. Autism Works CEO Peter MacDonald says about his company's software testing work:

It requires persistence, an eye for detail and methodical working without getting distracted. What can be quite boring tasks for most people play to the positive side of autism. We'll test, better, faster and deeper than other companies –

we won't be having the coffee machine conversations. (*Daily Telegraph* 2012)

Recognition of these strengths is welcome, but employers must not be allowed to see autistic workers as pushovers: uncomplaining people whom they can drive to work extra hard, at boring tasks, without breaks.

The European Disability Forum (2014) argues: 'Employer[s] need to…discourage competition because collaborative work is more effective than competitive.' Remove distressing rivalry at work by:

- scrapping systems that rank staff or judge them against each other

- negotiating and agreeing pay and conditions rather than incorporating any element of individual reward in them

- replacing performance-related pay with an increase in basic pay.

7. THE TROUBLE WITH MANAGERS

Paul Binks, who managed an autistic worker, advises other managers to 'never assume that you know best; consultation with the individual about their needs and what you can do to help them is essential' (Worton and Binks 2008, p.76). So the least an employer can do is to ensure that its managers:

- understand autism

- do not show favouritism

- communicate appropriately

- avoid disruptive supervision

- do not oversupervise or micromanage

- avoid gratuitous bossiness.

Some writers (e.g. Bissonnette 2013a, pp.65–68) argue that people with Asperger's Syndrome or autism have difficulty dealing with authority and advise us to submit to the established hierarchies. Perhaps instead, we could question the idea of authority at work: whether it is necessary, who holds it, how it is exercised. Beginning with training managers, holding them accountable and removing their excessive power, we could progress to reorganising work on a democratic, collective basis, with essential management tasks shared out or rotated appropriately among the workforce.

Managing performance

We all want the job done well. In many workplaces, this is probably best achieved by binning the current 'performance-management' regime and starting again. For autistic workers, getting help to do the job well may include:

- training, coaching, the right tools for the job

- regular meetings to identify and anticipate issues before problems arise:

   > I meet with my manager and my NAS support worker every month to discuss how work is going and any problems I might be having. When I started, the meetings were fortnightly, but after about a year, they became monthly. This has been very useful. At one time I was having problems with housing, which meant that I was stressed and tired, and having to take time off work. We discussed this at the regular meeting, and as a result, management referred me to counselling, which helped to resolve my difficulties. (Josh, data entry assistant)

- regular feedback in an agreed format and at an agreed venue and time

- the right to be accompanied by a union representative and/or support worker

- recognition that what the manager sees as a performance problem may actually be a different, even better, way of doing things

- recognition of the possibility that if the autistic worker did not carry out the instructions or obey the rules, it may be because those instructions or rules were unreasonable, not communicated clearly, or both

- awareness that the autistic worker may have anxiety, low self-esteem or previous experience of bullying, so may struggle with criticism.

The autistic manager?

Straightforward barrier removal: do not compel autistic workers to become managers if they feel unsuited, and do not allow any detriment to arise from this.

> [A]fter another run-in with a member of my staff left me in tears...I decided enough was enough and...plucked up the courage to tell my bosses about my diagnosis and to ask them [to]...remove my staff management responsibilities. A month later I have been 'staff-free' and pretty stress-free for the last two weeks! (Lynne 2015)

> They've suggested that I move into a lower grade to avoid taking on the new management duties, but that would mean a pay cut. (Liza, railway station supervisor)

8. BULLYING, HARASSMENT, DISCRIMINATION

Applying the principle that 'prevention is better than cure', strive to prevent bullying and harassment by raising awareness of what they are, the harm they cause and advice on what someone can do if they experience or witness them.

Attack bullying and harassment with a comprehensive, negotiated policy, explicitly including autism and neurological diversity – one that works in practice rather than just looking good on paper. Key elements will include:

- designated people to contact, trained for the role

- confidentiality

- taking complaints seriously: not 'oh, that's just banter' or 'lighten up'

- choice for complainants over how their complaint is pursued; they may want informal resolution rather than formal discipline, or vice versa

- keeping the two parties away from each other while the issue is dealt with: in most cases, by moving the accused rather than the accuser

- helping a target of bullying or harassment to deal with its impact: counselling, support

- no disciplinary action for any sickness absence caused by bullying and/or harassment.

Autism-Europe (2014, p.33) points out that to assert their right to complain or submit a grievance, autistic workers may need support in understanding their rights, communicating grievances and participating in the grievance process and that the person dealing with the grievance also needs to be aware of autism. So it is crucial that the policy gives the complainant (and the accused) the right to full representation throughout. This may include a specialist autism support worker as well as a trade union representative. To fulfil their role effectively, trade unions may elect specific bullying and harassment reps. Both these and regular union reps will benefit from appropriate training, with the union providing it and the employer allowing paid time off work for reps to attend.

An effective trade union will recognise that where there is an individual grievance there is usually a collective problem. So, when a member experiences bullying, harassment or discrimination, it will demand justice for that member and will also insist that the employer address the issue of how this came about and what actions it will take to prevent a recurrence.

As for straightforward discrimination and abuse like Andrew and Adam (see Chapter 2) were subjected to: don't do it or tolerate it.

9. ALL CHANGE!

To minimise day-to-day disruption, an autistic worker may benefit from:

- a personal workstation or desk, away from busier areas

- sameness where practical – for example regular break times, the same parking space, the same seat in meetings

- no unannounced or compulsory overtime

- meetings at regular times

- practical procedures to follow in the event of problems – for example, ensuring that a secondary printer is available, should the regular printer fail.

Changes to ways of working will be easier if:

- they only happen when necessary or beneficial

- they are negotiated between the employer and the trade union

- the bargaining agenda includes equalities, including disability and neurodiversity

- criteria for selecting who is to be moved, promoted, redeployed and so forth are negotiated, transparent and objective

- individual circumstances, including autism, are taken into account

- reasonable adjustments are made for the change process and for the new role

- workers have the right to appeal against a change to their work role or location

- once change is agreed, adequate notice is given in appropriate formats.

In strongly unionised workplaces there is almost always an agreed procedure for change that incorporates some or all of these points. In non-unionised workplaces, the employer is more likely to impose change with little consultation or notice, to the detriment of autistic and other workers.

Autism-Europe points out that while autistic people's difficulties with change should be respected, this should not be a pretext for denying opportunities for career advancement. Moreover, it is important to maintain autistic workers' support structures during periods of change and to recognise that support needs may be greater (Autism-Europe 2014, p.31).

10. JOB INSECURITY IN A TIME OF AUSTERITY

Austerity-driven policies create significant barriers to autistic workers. Removing these barriers means adopting an alternative to austerity.

Instead of cutting services and jobs, an alternative would expand public services that both meet needs and create jobs. Autistic people need more services – diagnosis, support workers, learning support assistants, job coaches and more – and more jobs across the public services will mean more jobs for autistic workers.

Public-sector jobs are generally more secure and accountable and less profit-driven than private-sector jobs. However, those in 'caring' roles are notoriously underpaid and understaffed. This can damage morale and cause high staff turnover, so autistic clients have to deal with stressed and frequently changing support workers. More staff with higher wages and better conditions will mean both a better service and a better working environment for autistic people. Nurse Jules says: 'They need to recruit more nurses so we do not work alone in an overloading environment.'

Instead of unpaid, low-paid, zero-hours, agency, fixed-term or otherwise casual employment, autistic people need secure work with decent pay and conditions and guaranteed hours. Autistic people do not need to be pushed into unsuitable work. If there is no suitable job available for an autistic person, then she is entitled to receive an income and support from the society that has failed to provide her with a suitable job.

There is always an alternative to cutting jobs, even where a work process has become obsolete or less labour-intensive. Expanding production or services, or sharing out the remaining work by scrapping overtime and/or cutting hours (without cutting pay) can keep the same number of jobs. In the UK, trade unions have the statutory right to propose alternatives to redundancy.

Where redundancies are made, transparent, objective criteria and selection processes that adopt many of the principles argued for in this book will minimise disadvantage and discrimination against autistic workers. In many countries, the law requires employers to observe equality provisions when selecting workers for redundancy. For example, the UK's Equality Act and the US's Americans With Disabilities Act offer protection to disabled workers against unfair criteria and processes.

Chapter 4

Autism, Work and the Law

A GLOBAL CONVENTION FOR RIGHTS

The United Nations Convention on the Rights of Persons with Disabilities (UNCRPD) is an international human rights treaty acknowledged as a major step forward in the worldwide perception of disabled people as equal citizens with human rights rather than as objects of pity. Adopted by the UN General Assembly in 2006, the Convention came into force in 2008.

The UNCRPD bases itself on the social model of disability – disabled people's representatives were involved in writing it. It recognises in its preamble that 'disability results from the interaction between persons with impairments and attitudinal barriers that hinders their full and effective participation in society on an equal basis with others'. The preamble also emphasises that disability discrimination violates human dignity. It stresses the importance of both individual autonomy and active involvement in decision making by disabled people. The Convention's stated purpose is 'to promote, protect and ensure the full and equal enjoyment of all human rights and fundamental freedoms to all persons with disabilities'.

It falls to 'State Parties' (mostly, national governments) to make these fine-sounding principles happen in practice. As of September 2015, the Convention had 159 signatories and 157 parties, including 156 states and the European Union (EU).

When a State Party ratifies the Convention, it confirms that it will abide by the standards set in it. Each State Party must report on its progress in implementing the Convention within two years of enforcing it and every four years thereafter.

The UNCRPD obliges its signatories to 'promote recognition of the skills, merits and abilities of persons with disabilities and of their contributions to the workforce and the labour market'. Article 27, on work and employment, includes disabled people's rights to freedom from discrimination; equal pay, opportunities and working conditions; trade union rights; and help in finding and keeping work.

EUROPEAN UNION

The EU ratified the UNCRPD in 2010 and shares responsibility for its implementation with national governments. Although most EU member states have ratified the Convention, Autism-Europe (2014, p.17) describes the degree of its implementation as 'diverse', particularly regarding employment, adding that 'even where sound legislation is in place, discrimination against people with autism…still occurs and significant barriers to their participation in the workforce continue'. The UN has urged the EU to adopt a European Accessibility Act and take other measures to improve its implementation of the Convention (European Disability Forum 2015).

Article 15 of the European Social Charter states: 'Disabled persons have the right to vocational training, rehabilitation and resettlement.' In 2000, the EU's Employment Equality Framework Directive 2000/78/EC required member states to develop legislation to stop discrimination against disabled people in employment and training. However, Autism-Europe (2014, p.17) argues that 'the scope of this directive does not provide adequate redress for the discrimination in employment that is commonly faced by people with autism' and advocates a new, broader, more effective directive.

Before this, in 1996 the European Parliament adopted as a Written Declaration the Charter for Persons with Autism previously adopted by Autism-Europe. It includes the rights to:

• a sufficient income or wage

• meaningful employment and training.

UNITED KINGDOM

The UK signed and ratified the UNCRPD in 2009 but has opted out of parts on education, immigration, social security and the armed forces.

The UK's Disability Discrimination Acts (DDA) of 1995 and 2006 were consolidated in the Equality Act 2010. The Labour government added the 'Equality Duty' to the DDA in 2006, which was retained in the Equality Act. This is a duty on all organisations carrying out public functions to challenge discrimination, involve disabled people in relevant decision making and to take positive steps to promote inclusion and equality. This includes nearly all public-sector bodies, but far fewer private companies. The Equality Duty pushed UK legislation in the direction of a social model approach but the 2010–15 Conservative/LibDem coalition government weakened the duty significantly, 'reducing its usefulness as a way for disabled people to take forward their rights through public policy' (Trade Union Congress 2015).

Autism became the first disability to have its own specific legislation in the UK. The ASD Strategic Action Plan for Wales, launched in 2008, is generally recognised as the world's first national autism strategy. It was followed by the Autism Act, applying to England and Wales, in 2009 and the Scottish Strategy for Autism and the Autism Act Northern Ireland in 2011.

The Autism Act is very short, simply requiring the Secretary of State for Health to produce a strategy for adults with autism and statutory guidance for local authorities and local health bodies. Neither the Act, the Strategy, nor the statutory guidance places legal obligations on employers (except for local and health authorities and only as service providers). The UK government evaluated the progress of the Act in 2011 and 'refreshed' it in 2014 (Department of Health 2011, 2014). Although the updated Strategy recognises that each autistic adult wants 'support to get a job and support from my employer to help me keep it' (Department of Health 2014, p.7), it still places no specific statutory obligations on employers. While government minister Norman Lamb MP described the Strategy in 2014 as 'fundamentally sound', Autistic-UK (2014) called it 'fundamentally flawed', arguing that it 'has had little appreciable effect on the lives of the majority of English autistic people'.

UNITED STATES OF AMERICA

While the US has signed the UN Convention, its Senate voted in December 2012 not to ratify it. A conservative faction of Republican Senators opposed the ratification and the vote fell six short of the two-thirds majority required.

The significant legislation for autistic workers in the US is the Americans with Disabilities Act (ADA). The section on employment (Title I) states that qualified applicants with disabilities may not be discriminated against at any stage of their employment from application onwards and requires employers to make reasonable accommodations.

Section 503 of the Rehabilitation Act 1973 places extra requirement on employers with federal contracts to hire, retain and promote disabled workers.

CANADA

Canada has ratified the UNCRPD. Discrimination on grounds of disability is unlawful in both federal and provincial law, at all stages from recruitment onwards. Workers are protected by human rights laws and codes. Employers must make reasonable accommodations for disabled workers, must provide a healthy work environment and must take steps to prevent discrimination and harassment.

AUSTRALIA

Australia has ratified the UNCRPD. The main relevant law in Australia is the Disability Discrimination Act, which outlaws discrimination (direct and indirect) and harassment and requires employers to make reasonable adjustments.

TEN KEY LEGAL CONCEPTS

1. Does an autistic person count as disabled under the law?

The UN Convention states: 'Persons with disabilities include those who have long-term physical, mental, intellectual or sensory impairments which in interaction with various barriers may hinder their full and effective participation in society on an equal basis with others.' Most national legislation does not list impairments or conditions that qualify a person as disabled under the law, instead requiring the individual to show what he cannot do: a 'medical model' approach based on individual shortcomings rather than social barriers.

The US ADA defines a 'individual with a disability' as a person who has a physical or mental impairment that substantially limits one or more major life activities, has a record of such an impairment, or is regarded as having such an impairment.

Under the UK's Equality Act, a person has a disability if he has a physical or mental impairment that has a substantial and long-term adverse effect on his ability to carry out normal day-to-day activities.

It is not necessary to have a diagnosis to qualify as disabled. Whether an autistic person counts as disabled will be considered on a case-by-case basis but the following suggest that, in the UK, in nearly every case, he will.

The Government Equalities Office (GEO) lists 'autistic spectrum disorders' as an example of impairment from which disability may arise and gives a hypothetical example of a man with Asperger Syndrome struggling to understand instructions given during office banter (Office for Disability Issues 2011, pp.9, 41).

The GEO also lists 'factors which, if they are experienced by a person, *it would be reasonable* to regard as having a substantial adverse effect on day-to-day activities', including many that are often associated with autism: for example, difficulty adapting to minor changes in routine; wanting to avoid people; persistent distractibility (Office for Disability Issues 2011, pp.53–55, emphasis original).

Hewett v Motorola [2004] IRLR 545 provides case law: the Employment Appeals Tribunal found that Mr Hewett, who has Asperger Syndrome, was disabled under the law because of his difficulty understanding social interaction.

The Equality and Human Rights Commission's Code of Practice (Equality and Human Rights Commission 2011, para 6.9, p.80), to which employers must have regard, states:

> In order to avoid discrimination, it would be sensible for employers not to attempt to make a fine judgment as to whether a particular individual falls within the statutory definition of disability, but to focus instead on meeting the needs of each worker.

In Northern Ireland, a joint government and voluntary sector guide advises employers: 'There is no doubt that most people with autism will meet [the UK legal] definition' (NAS, DEL, ECNI, EFDNI 2011, p.11).

The US Equal Employment Opportunity Commission (EEOC) advises that it will 'easily be concluded that…autism substantially limits brain function' and that it will therefore be considered a disability (Equal Employment Opportunity Commission 2011, §1630.2).

2. Discrimination

The UN Convention defines discrimination on the grounds of disability as any distinction, exclusion or restriction on the basis of disability that has the purpose or effect of impairing or nullifying the recognition, enjoyment or exercise, on an equal basis with others, of all human rights and fundamental freedoms in the political, social, cultural, civil or any other field.

The US Department of Labor gives examples of discrimination at work: limiting or classifying an applicant or employee in an adverse way; denying employment to someone who is qualified; or not advancing (promoting) employees with disabilities (Pacelli 2014, p.45).

In the UK, the following actions by an employer are unlawful under the Equality Act 2010:

- Direct discrimination. A directly discriminates against B if, because of a protected characteristic (for the purposes of this book, disability by reason of autism), A treats B less favourably than A treats or would treat others. For example, if an employer were to say, 'I'm dismissing you because you're autistic' or 'I'm not giving you a bonus unlike the rest of the staff because you're autistic' or 'I'm not promoting you because you're autistic', that would constitute direct discrimination. In addition, direct discrimination includes less favourable treatment towards someone because of:

  - association with someone who is disabled – for example dismissing an employee because he has an autistic child

  - perception of disability – for example an employer dismissing an employee because he thinks the employee is autistic.

- Indirect discrimination. This occurs where A applies a provision, criterion or practice to everyone but it disadvantages a particular group of people who share a particular protected characteristic, and A cannot justify it. For example, an employer requires staff to attend a yearly team-building weekend, stating that their performance during the weekend will inform their pay rise. John performs badly in the team-building exercises because of his autism. He is therefore disadvantaged by the policy, as would be other autistic people. Given that there are many ways that would better inform a pay rise, the employer is unlikely to be able to justify its policy.

- Discrimination arising from disability. A discriminates against B if A treats B unfavourably because of something arising in consequence of B's disability and A cannot show that the treatment is a proportionate means of achieving a legitimate aim. For example, an employer dismisses an autistic worker because he rocks on his chair at work, even though he performs adequately in his job. However, there is no protection for the disabled worker here if A shows that A did not know and could not reasonably have been expected to know that B had a disability.

In Australia, direct discrimination, indirect discrimination and aiding and abetting discrimination are unlawful. Under 'vicarious liability' provisions, employers are liable for unlawful discrimination by their agents or employees.

3. Positive action

The legal bar on discrimination does not prevent employers implementing positive measures to assist disabled workers.

The UK's Disability Discrimination Act allowed a wider range of positive action measures than other anti-discrimination laws. It is, for example, lawful to reserve a job vacancy for a disabled person, or to guarantee an interview to disabled people and to make an adjustment that treats a disabled worker more favourably than a non-disabled worker.

4. Reasonable accommodation/adjustment

The UN Convention defines 'reasonable accommodation' as 'necessary and appropriate modification and adjustments not imposing a disproportionate or undue burden, where needed in a particular case, to ensure to persons with disabilities the enjoyment or exercise on equal basis with others of all human rights and fundamental freedoms'.

The EU Directive 2000/78/EC instructs member states to ensure that employers make reasonable accommodations for disabled workers. Autism-Europe reports (2014, p.14) that 'while all European countries now have such legislation in place, the impact of this directive remains limited in practice'.

While most countries use the term 'reasonable accommodations', UK and Australian law uses the term 'reasonable adjustments'. The US ADA requires employers to make reasonable accommodations.

Many of the measures advocated in the previous chapter of this book would count as reasonable accommodations/ adjustments. The UK's Equality and Human Rights Commission provides examples of reasonable adjustments.

Refusal to make reasonable accommodations/adjustments is unlawful discrimination. An employer may defend its refusal to make an accommodation that a worker wants by arguing that it is not reasonable. The EU Directive excuses employers from making accommodations that place a 'disproportionate burden'; Autism-Europe argues (2014, p.17) that this allows employers a simple way out of making accommodations for, or even hiring, an autistic worker. US law exempts measures that cause undue hardship or interfere with productivity; UK law allows employers to refuse to make adjustments on the grounds of effectiveness, practicality or cost; Australian employers may lawfully refuse to make adjustments that cause 'unjustifiable hardship' in terms of costs and disadvantages to others.

5. Disclosure and confidentiality

In the UK, US and most other countries, an applicant or worker is not legally obliged to disclose whether he is autistic. However, many of the legal rights outlined in this chapter are only accessible to people who have told their employer that they are disabled. There remains a risk that if a person does disclose his autism, the employer may mistreat him under a different pretext: it can be very difficult to prove discrimination.

In the UK, Section 60 of the Equality Act bars prospective employers from asking questions about applicants' health before offering the job, except in specified circumstances, including to establish whether the applicant 'will be able to carry out a function that is intrinsic to the work concerned'.

In the US, recent changes to Section 503 of the Rehabilitation Act prohibit medical enquiries before a job is offered, allowing only questions about the applicants' ability to carry out the job. After making a job offer, an employer may ask medical and disability-related questions, so long as it asks the same questions to everyone offered the same kind of job. Once an employee has started work, the employer may not ask disability-related questions unless they are 'job related and consistent with business necessity'. An employer may not rescind a job offer because the applicant discloses a disability.

In Australia, it is unlawful for an employer to ask for information that may be used to discriminate against a person on the basis of disability but it is lawful to ask for the same information from all applicants and to ask for information if the disability is linked to job tasks.

6. Bullying

In many countries, workplace bullying is not explicitly unlawful. In Europe, bullying usually falls under general laws about health and safety at work, although Denmark, France, the Netherlands, Norway and Sweden have specific laws against bullying.

Most Canadian jurisdictions have legislation about workplace violence and/or harassment. Where there is no legislation that specifically addresses bullying, the general duty clause establishes the duty of employers to protect employees from risks at work (Canadian Centre for Occupational Health and Safety 2014).

In the US, supporters of the Healthy Workplace Bill, including unions, are campaigning for a national law against workplace bullying and intimidation. As of September 2015, 29 US states and two Territories have introduced the Bill.

Australia's Victoria state made workplace bullying a criminal offence in 2011 with 'Brodie's Law', named after a young woman who killed herself after being bullied by work colleagues. Trade unions and others are campaigning to extend it to other Australian states.

7. Harassment

In the UK, the law defines harassment as unwanted conduct related to a protected characteristic (for the purposes of this book, disability by reason of autism) with the purpose or effect of violating the target's dignity or creating an intimidating, hostile, degrading, humiliating or offensive environment for the victim. This could include jokes about autism or imitating an autistic worker in a derogatory fashion.

As with direct discrimination, it is possible for A to harass B owing to their association with an autistic person. For example, George is regularly humiliated at work by colleagues who make fun of the fact that he has an autistic son. Similarly, it is possible for an individual to suffer harassment based on perception: for example, A harasses B because A thinks B is autistic.

In the US, harassment on the grounds of disability is unlawful under the 1964 Civil Rights Act and the 1990 Americans with Disabilities Act.

The difficulty facing an autistic person who is harassed is that even if he has the courage and support to take legal action, it may be hard to prove that the harasser mistreated him because he is autistic. Autistic workers are often harassed (or bullied) by managers or colleagues who do not know they are autistic but pick on them for being 'weird'.

8. Victimisation

Although in common parlance, 'victimisation' means picking on someone, it has a specific, narrower meaning in employment law: subjecting a person to a detriment because that person has done or may do a protected act.

The UK's Equality Act specifies four protected acts:

- bringing proceedings under the Act

- giving evidence or information in connection with proceedings under the Act

- doing any other thing for the purposes of or in connection with the Act

- making an allegation that A or another person has contravened the Act.

For example, Tina is sacked when she raises a grievance that she has been discriminated against because of her autism. Raising the grievance would be the protected act and dismissal would be the detriment.

9. Health, safety and welfare

Some aspects of a country's health, safety and/or welfare law impact on autistic people's working conditions and rights. For example, it may be helpful to:

- conduct a workplace risk assessment, or to ensure that existing risk assessments do not assume neurotypicality

- check regulations about provision of rest facilities

- check working-time regulations

- ensure that staff health-and-safety representatives are aware of and exercise their rights.

10. Trade union rights

The UN Convention explicitly includes trade union rights among the rights that must be upheld for disabled people. The EU's Social Charter upholds the right of workers to organise and to engage in collective bargaining with employers.

Under international and most national laws, workers have the right to join a trade union (known in some countries as a 'labor union') and not to be sacked, or caused other detriment, for exercising their right to do so. Under certain circumstances, the employer must recognise the trade union for the purposes of representing members individually and collectively. International legal principles uphold the right of workers, through their trade unions, to take strike action, although the laws governing how this must be carried out vary between different countries.

In the UK, workers have the right to be accompanied by a trade union representative to:

- disciplinary meetings

- grievance meetings

- meetings to discuss applications for flexible working

- some other meetings.

Trade union representatives have certain rights in order to exercise their role. There is more information about the role of trade unions in the next chapter.

Chapter 5

Organising for Change

If autistic people are to achieve equality and to realise our right to suitable, rewarding work, then employment practices must change radically. This book has so far argued that it is workplaces rather than autistic workers that must change and has examined, in some detail, the barriers that exist and the changes that might remove or reduce them. The remaining question is 'how will change come about?'

Employers could change their practices. A few may be trying to do so. We can hope that a few more will but if we wait for employers to make their workplaces autism friendly voluntarily we will be waiting a long time – far longer than a fair society would expect anyone to wait for progress and equality.

Autism-Europe (2014, p.55) advocates some steps:

- further research into autism and employment

- sharing good practices

- networking between employers of autistic workers

- linking autistic job seekers to potential employers.

Governments can help advance equality and access by placing more specific and demanding legal obligations on employers to make workplaces autism friendly.

Governments are best placed to do this in their own capacity as employers. The more services and industries are kept in, or brought into, public ownership, the more effective this can be:

- When an industry or service is publicly owned, the government (whether national, provincial/state/regional, or local) has more direct power to impose progressive policies.

- Public ownership also allows for more direct democratic public input through elected, accountable representatives.

- Removal of the profit motive through public ownership means that considerations such as equality and access can take a higher priority. Changes and adjustments can become 'reasonable' or practical when cost is not the overwhelmingly decisive factor.

If we wait for governments to act, we may have a long wait! To compel employers and governments to act and to make the change ourselves, we need to mobilise a movement. Why?

- Because this book is not (and does not claim or try to be) the last word on autism-friendly workplaces. A movement can identify more barriers and thence promote more radical, thoroughgoing and effective changes.

- The process of articulating, organising and collective campaigning is itself empowering for autistic people, as it is generally for people engaging in a collective struggle to improve their lives.

- A movement will test the boundaries of how far we can go within our existing society and establish what more fundamental changes we need.

- A movement can monitor the actions of employers, governments and quangos, making sure that they do not continue to present us with inaccessible and intolerable working conditions while incorporating the language of autism equality, ticking boxes and obtaining Kitemarks.

- As the UK's National Autistic Society (2012, p.4) insists: 'Campaigning is critical if people with autism and their families are to get a better deal from society and from the existing services that are there to support them.'

A PROGRESSIVE WORKPLACE POLICY

Workplaces can progress towards becoming more autism friendly by adopting a policy on autism and neurological diversity. A good policy would include:

- a commitment to applying the social model of disability to autism

- recognition that the population and therefore the workforce is neurologically diverse

- involvement of autistic workers in developing, implementing and monitoring the policy through their representative trade unions

- identifying barriers to autistic workers' participation (such as those in Chapter 2)

- identifying ways to remove or reduce those barriers (such as those in Chapter 3)

- a commitment to develop policy on other neurodivergent conditions, such as dyslexia and ADHD

- continuous review of the barriers and the facility to identify further barriers

- continuous monitoring of the measures taken to reduce the barriers and the facility to identify new measures.

COLLECTIVE BARGAINING AND TRADE UNIONS

The workplace's autism and neurodiversity policy will be most effective if it is negotiated between the employer and the workers through their trade union – if it is an agreement rather than a diktat. This will help to ensure that:

- the policy is acceptable to the workforce, including autistic workers

- it does not contain provisions that disadvantage workers or strengthen management's hand against the workforce

- it is in line with the union's policies

- union members, especially autistic members, are represented in the process of drawing up the policy

- any changes to and development of the policy also have to be negotiated and agreed.

Effective negotiations will centre around the points in the previous section. In particular, they will seek to identify and remove barriers, rather than treat autism as a medical problem and autistic workers as people to be pitied.

If the employer is unwilling or reluctant to consider a policy, the union may need to exert pressure by campaigning or even industrial action.

Trade unions are bodies of workers that collectively organise to defend and extend workers' rights, conditions and interests. At their best, they are not so much organisations that speak for workers but organisations through which workers speak for themselves.

Unions can represent individual autistic members (and members with caring responsibility for autistic dependants).

I had a union adviser with me at all the sessions and panel hearings. They stuck up for me and seemed confident that I could be moved to another position with the organisation, but HR said that there were no vacancies. I applied to Employment Tribunal with the union's support and the employer settled out of court. (Lauren, civil service scientist)

> Having a union representative with you is so much better, because if I had been on my own, I might have broken down again. I think unions are very supportive in that respect, but more needs to be done so that more people in the union understand about autism. (Syed, railway track engineer)

Unions can organise and mobilise union members in support of workmates who are facing discrimination or unfair treatment at work.

Mo works in a ticket office and has an autistic daughter who needs a predictable home routine. Mo's roster included variable shifts. He applied for 'flexible working' to have regular hours, but his manager was hostile. A trade union representative accompanied him to all meetings. Union members organised a petition of his workmates supporting Mo's fixed-hours arrangement and said that they were willing to take industrial action in support of him. When the manager tried to cancel the fixed-hours arrangement, the union appealed to a higher level manager and had Mo's hours restored to what he needed.

Autistic worker Caroline (2014) argues that 'for many years the trade union movement has been fighting for disabled workers and our carers to have rights at work', highlighting that unions give disabled people a voice at conferences, campaign for legal protection against discrimination and offer legal support. She concludes: 'The union movement is well aware that autistic workers need a voice and the best things about trade unions is that they are experts on empowering people who aren't getting a fair deal.' Civil servant Austin describes how being involved in the union has benefited him:

> I strongly believe that without the union, I wouldn't be where I am, or in any job at all. The branch chair mentored me and my own personal case gave me experience which I can apply when dealing with members. Because of this, now I feel like a person of worth and value. I've been on the TUC (Trade Union Congress) delegation and spoken at

conferences a number of times. So I feel like I have been properly developed.

Trade unions will be most effective in promoting autistic workers' interests if they have structures through which autistic members can organise and articulate their concerns. For autistic workers, it is easiest to organise through the workers' organisations that already exist: trade unions.

Four-fifths of UK trade unionists are members of unions that have disabled members' structures. More unions are (somewhat belatedly) setting up these structures and there has been an increase in the proportion of unions taking steps to encourage disabled workers to join and actively become involved in the union (Trade Union Congress 2015).

Unions, though, still have much room for improvement. They can become more effective and more autism friendly through:

- organising
  - recruiting and mobilising workers in autism services
  - producing recruitment materials aimed at autistic workers and carers
  - using 'know-your-rights' guides to make workers confident about demanding their rights through collective union organisation
- communicating effectively
  - ensuring that union materials are clear and accurate
  - using a variety of formats – such as graphics, cartoons and videos as well as words
  - not allowing union meetings to become dominated by jargon and cliquey banter
- fighting austerity
  - defending autism services from cuts
  - ensuring that protests are autism friendly where possible

- structures for members

  - ensuring that the union has representative structures for disabled members

  - ensuring that these structures have resources and power to organise and are not just 'talking shops'

  - publicising these structures and their activities so that autistic members know that they are welcome to get involved

- making union events and meetings autism friendly

  - giving meetings a clear agenda and running them to time as far as possible

  - making procedures clear

  - keeping good order in the meeting

  - considering meeting venues, particularly regarding sensory issues

  - considering help with carers' costs to enable members with autistic dependants to attend

- providing training

  - running Autism in the Workplace courses (contact the author for information)

  - making sure that the union's training is autism friendly

- promoting understanding, tackling ignorance

  - displaying materials at work that promote greater understanding of autism

  - educating members about language and challenging unkind or inappropriate comments at work and at union events

- holding discussions at union events, perhaps inviting speakers.

An important cross-union body is the (UK) TUC Disabled Workers' Conference and Committee. The Conference, which brings together delegates from many trade unions each year, passed a resolution on Autism in the Workplace in 2013 and the Committee has published a handbook (Booth 2014) and supports training and campaigning for autism-friendly workplaces.

The bottom line is this: trade unions are working-class organisations and the working class is neurologically diverse. To be effective, trade unions must unite all workers and overcome division and discrimination. A better understanding of autism and neurodiversity will enable trade unions to defend their members more effectively. It will also enable them to involve and mobilise more members by ensuring that union culture and procedures are not unnecessarily geared towards a narrowly defined neurotypicality. That will benefit all workers.

NOTHING ABOUT US WITHOUT US

This subheading is an important slogan of the disabled people's movement, a challenge to the years of decisions and policies being made for us and often against our wishes and interests. Ari Ne'eman, President of the US Autistic Self Advocacy Network, cautions against imposing 'normalcy' in autistic people. Instead, he advocates allowing cognitively disabled people to communicate their own needs (*Independent* 2012).

The UN Convention on the Rights of Persons with Disabilities, Article 4.3, states: 'In…decision-making processes concerning issues relating to persons with disabilities, States Parties shall involve persons with disabilities, including children with disabilities, through their representative organisations.' However, this has not necessarily happened in reality. In the UK, the only voluntary organisation invited to join the Autism Programme Board – charged with overseeing the implementation of the Autism Act – was the National Autistic Society, which is not (and does not claim to be) a representative organisation of autistic people.

Moreover, what consultation there is may have limited usefulness. Kabie Brook, chairperson of Autism Rights Group Highland, says:

> Often we are not getting our voices heard and there is a huge disparity between what is being said and what is being heard. Tokenism is rife, it can often feel as if autistic people are only included because it is necessary to tick a box, that it is being done for the process rather than any usable or actionable output. (Wheeler 2015a)

Brook adds:

> The autistic rights movement is really in its infancy. Autistic people's organisations are few and we do not hold senior or influential posts in the organisations that claim to represent and support us. By that I mean the large corporate charities that are still 'for' rather than 'by' us, although hopefully we are seeing very small changes there.

Medical professionals and some charities provide useful services and resources for autistic people and for those supporting them. However, while some may campaign in the interests of autistic people, this does not necessarily mean that they speak for autistic people. Twenty-four organisations joined the Autistic Self Advocacy Network in publishing a joint letter (Autistic Self Advocacy Network, The Association for Autistic Community, Autism Women's Network, Association of Programs for Rural Independent Living *et al.* 2014) to the sponsors of the US charity Autism Speaks, explaining that it does not represent autistic people and accusing it of systematically excluding autistic people from its leadership.

Moreover, some charities have come into conflict with trade unions and/or pursue policies that are at odds with those of trade unions. For example, the National Autistic Society sponsors several 'free schools', which teaching unions oppose.

Long-standing disability activists and writers Michael Oliver and Colin Barnes (2012, p.169) argue that the resurgence of large charities since the mid-2000s mirrors the declining influence of the disabled people's movement. However, there is still a disabled people's movement and there is still a trade union movement. In this writer's view, a revival and alliance of solidarity between the two carries the best hope for achieving the just transformation of workplaces proposed by this book.

References

AGCAS Disability Task Group (2010–2011) *What Happened Next? A Report on the First Destinations of 2009/2010 Disabled Graduates.* Sheffield: AGCAS.

Ambitious about Autism (2011) *Education System Failing Young People with Autism when they Leave School.* Press release, 17 October. London: AAA.

Attwood, T. (2007) *The Complete Guide to Asperger's Syndrome.* London: Jessica Kingsley Publishers.

Australian Government (2015) *How to Support Job Seekers with Autism.* JobAccess. Accessed 25 October 2015 at www.jobaccess.gov.au/service-providers/assisting-job-seekers/supporting-job-seekers-different-ty/learningintellectual-a-0.

Autism-Europe (2011) 'Belgian cooperative employs the unique skills of people with high functioning autism.' *Link 56,* 14–15.

Autism-Europe (2014) *Autism and Work: Together We Can.* Brussels: Autism-Europe.

Autistic Self Advocacy Network, The Association for Autistic Community, Autism Women's Network, Association of Programs for Rural Independent Living *et al.* (2014) *Joint Letter to the Sponsors of Autism Speaks.* ASAN. Accessed 25 October 2015 at www.autisticadvocacy.org/2014/01/2013-joint-letter-to-the-sponsors-of-autism-speaks.

Autistic-UK (2014) 'Let us contribute to a workable autism strategy.' *The New Idealist: The Autism Issue 6,* 11.

Bancroft, K., Batten, A., Lambert, S. and Madders, T. (2012) *The Way We Are: Autism in 2012.* London: National Autistic Society.

Barker, K. (2015) 'Interior design.' *Your Autism 49,* 2, 23.

BBC (2009) *Disabled Man Bullied with Helmet.* BBC. Accessed 25 October 2015 at http://news.bbc.co.uk/1/hi/england/manchester/8156396.stm.

BBC (2012) *Autistic Chef 'Exploited' by Plymouth's Astor Hotel.* BBC. Accessed 25 October 2015 at www.bbc.co.uk/news/uk-england-devon-17317077.

Beard, E. (2008) 'I'm Just So Willing to Work.' In G. Edmonds and L. Beardon (eds) *Asperger Syndrome and Employment.* London: Jessica Kingsley Publishers.

Bissonnette, B. (2013a) *Asperger's Syndrome Workplace Survival Guide.* London: Jessica Kingsley Publishers.

Bissonnette, B. (2013b) *The Complete Guide to Getting a Job for People with Asperger's Syndrome.* London: Jessica Kingsley Publishers.

Booth, J. (2013) *Plundering London Underground.* London: Merlin Press.

Booth, J. (2014) *Autism in the Workplace.* TUC. Accessed 25 October 2015 at www.tuc.org.uk/sites/default/files/Autism.pdf.

Brown, A. (2008) 'Experiences of Employment and Stress Before My Diagnosis of Asperger Syndrome.' In G. Edmonds and L. Beardon (eds) *Asperger Syndrome and Employment.* London: Jessica Kingsley Publishers.

Buckley, B. (2015) *Submission on National Disability Employment Framework.* Autism Asperger's Advocacy Australia. Canberra: A4.

Canadian Centre for Occupational Health and Safety (2014) *Bullying in the Workplace.* Accessed 25 October 2015 at www.ccohs.ca/oshanswers/psychosocial/bullying.html.

Caroline (2014) 'You have rights at work.' *Asperger United 79,* 6.

Cathy (2015) 'Letter.' *Asperger United 82,* 17.

Charlotte (2013) 'Letter.' *Asperger United 74,* 6.

Daily Telegraph (2012) 'Social Enterprise with Added Ambition; Entrepreneur Targets People with Autism for Software-Testing Venture.' June 5.

David (2013) Work. *Asperger United 74,* 4–5.

Department for Work and Pensions and National Autistic Society (2012) *Untapped Talent: A Guide to Employing People with Autism.* London: DWP/NAS.

Department of Health (2010) *Fulfilling and Rewarding Lives: the Strategy for Adults with Autism in England.* London: DoH.

Department of Health (2011) *Fulfilling and Rewarding Lives: The Strategy for Adults with Autism: Evaluating Progress.* London: DoH.

Department of Health (2014) *Think Autism: Fulfilling and Rewarding Lives, The Strategy for Adults with Autism in England: An Update.* London: DoH.

Edmonds, G. and Beardon, L. (eds) (2008) *Asperger Syndrome and Employment.* London: Jessica Kingsley Publishers.

Eleni (2013) 'Letter.' *Asperger United 73,* 10.

Equal Employment Opportunity Commission (2011) *EEOC Regulations to Implement the Equal Employment Provisions of the Americans with Disabilities Act.* Washington DC: EEOC.

Equality and Human Rights Commission (2011) *Equality Act 2010 Code of Practice, Employment.* Norwich: TSO.

European Disability Forum (2014) *eSkills for All.* Autism-Europe. Accessed on 26 October 2015 at www.autismeurope.org/files/files/eskills-for-all-pietro-brussels-11-02-2014.pdf.

European Disability Forum (2015) *United Nations Human Rights Recommendations to the EU.* Media release, 7 September.

The Guardian (2012) 'Loyal, Talented…Ignored: Employers Could Recruit a Whole Army of Unique Workers. But Ignorance and Fear Get in the Way.' 7 April.

Haggarty, M. (2008) 'Finding, Applying For and Starting a Job.' In G. Edmonds and L. Beardon (eds) *Asperger Syndrome and Employment.* London: Jessica Kingsley Publishers.

Health and Care Information Centre (2012) *Estimating the Prevalence of Autistic Spectrum Conditions in Adults.* Leeds: NHS.

Healthy Workplace Bill (2015) *The Problem.* Accessed 26 October 2015 at www.healthyworkplacebill.org/problem.php.

Heasley, S. (2014) *Work Environment May Improve Autism Symptoms. Disability Scoop.* Accessed 26 October 2015 at www.disabilityscoop.com/2014/01/15/work-autism-symptoms/19020.

House of Lords Hansard (2012) Question 738c9, Lord Toulig to Lord Hill of Oareford, 25 June.

Hughes, P. J. (2008) 'The Job Needs to Work for the Worker.' In G. Edmonds and L. Beardon (eds) *Asperger Syndrome and Employment.* London: Jessica Kingsley Publishers.

Independent (2012) 'World's First Autism Show Offers a Chance to Shine: Event Will Bring Disability into the Open and Celebrate its Links with Creativity.' June 16.

Jacqueline (2013) 'Letter.' *Asperger United 75,* 4–5.

Jarvis, S. (2008) 'What I have Learned from 25 Years of Employment.' In G. Edmonds and L. Beardon (eds) *Asperger Syndrome and Employment.* London: Jessica Kingsley Publishers.

Julie (2013a) 'Work part one.' *Asperger United 74,* 16–17.

Julie (2013b) 'Work part two.' *Asperger United 75,* 12–13.

REFERENCES

Lesco, S. (2011) *Employment and Asperger Syndrome.* Autism Research Institute. Accessed 26 October 2015 at www.autism.com/advocacy_lesco.

Lindsay (2012) *Simon Baron-Cohen Responds to Criticism from an Autistic Blogger – Part I.* Autist's Corner. Accessed 4 July 2015 at www.autistscorner.blogspot.co.uk/2011/09/simon-baron-cohen-responds-to-criticism.html.

Louisa (2015) 'Letter.' *Asperger United 81,* 15.

Lynne (2015) 'Late diagnosis.' *Asperger United 82,* 4–5.

Mark (2014) 'Throwing down one's locks.' *Asperger United 79,* 16–17.

Milton, D. (2012) '"Problems in living" and the mental well-being of people on the autism spectrum: part two.' *Asperger United 72,* 123.

Mostafa, M. (2015) 'Designs for living.' *Your Autism 49,* 2, 21–22.

National Autistic Society (2011) *What Next? Information for Adults with Autism Before and After Diagnosis.* London: NAS.

National Autistic Society (2012) *Act Together: A Step-by-Step Guide to Getting the Most out of the Autism Act.* London: NAS.

National Autistic Society (2015) *Support for Employment.* NAS. Accessed 26 October 2015 at www.autism.org.uk/working-with/support-for-employers.aspx.

National Autistic Society Northern Ireland, Department for Employment and Learning, Equality Commission for Northern Ireland, and Employers for Disability NI (2011) *Employing People with Autism: A Brief Guide for Employers.* Belfast: NAS, DEL, ECNI, EFDNI.

National Institute for Health and Clinical Excellence (2012) *The NICE Guideline on Recognition, Referral, Diagnosis and Management of Adults on the Autism Spectrum.* London: National Collaborating Centre for Mental Health.

Nick (2015) 'Book review.' *Asperger United 83,* 17.

Nishi, D. (2013) 'Take Your Search for a Job Offline.' *Wall Street Journal.* Accessed 26 October 2015 at www.wsj.com/articles/SB10001424127887323869604578368733437346820.

Office for Disability Issues (2011) *Guidance on Matters to be Taken into Account in Determining Questions Relating to the Definition of Disability.* London: ODI.

Oliver, M. and Barnes, C. (2012) *The New Politics of Disablement.* London: Palgrave Macmillan.

Pacelli, P. (2014) *Six Word Lessons for Autism Friendly Workplaces.* Washington: Pacelli Publishing.

Pring, J. (2014) '"Refreshed" Autism Strategy is All too Stale, Say Activists.' *Disability News Service.* Accessed 26 October 2015 at www.disabilitynewsservice.com/refreshed-autism-strategy-is-all-too-stale-say-activists.

Purkis, J. (2014) 'My Work Journey.' *Autism Women Matter.* Accessed 20 March 2015 at www.autismwomenmatter.com/employment/my-work-journey.

Purkis, J. (2015) 'What's Work and What's Home? Rules of Thumb versus Rules.' *Autism Women Matter.* Accessed 20 March 2015 at www.autismwomenmatter.com/employment/whats-work-and-whats-home-rules-of-thumb-versus-rules.

Redman, S., Downie, M., Rennison, R. and Batten, A. (2009). *Don't Write Me Off: Make the System Fair for People with Autism.* London: The National Autistic Society.

Richard (2013) 'The challenges of employment.' *Asperger United 74,* 12–13.

Sarah (2014) 'Letter.' *Asperger United 79,* 18.

Shattuck, P., Carter Narendorf. S., Cooper, B., Sterzing, P., Wagner, M. and Lounds Taylor, J. (2012) 'Postsecondary education and employment among youth with an autism spectrum disorder.' *Pediatrics 129,* 6, 1042–1049.

Shepherd, N. (2008) 'How Do You Communicate that You Have a Communication Problem…When You Have a Communication Problem?' In G. Edmonds and L. Beardon (eds) *Asperger Syndrome and Employment.* London: Jessica Kingsley Publishers.

Simone, R. (2010) *Asperger's on the Job.* Arlington TX: Future Horizons.

Slaughter, J. (2009) *Harassment: The Recession's Hidden Byproduct, Labor Notes.* Accessed 26 October 2015 at www.labornotes.org/2009/09/harassment-recession%e2%80%99s-hidden-byproduct.

SPICe (2010) *Briefing: Autism (Scotland) Bill.* Edinburgh: The Scottish Parliament.

Spillane, R. (2012) 'Why Workplaces Must Resist the Cult of Personality Testing.' Accessed 19 February 2016 at http://theconversation.com/why-workplaces-must-resist-the-cult-of-personality-testing-5540.

Sullings, N. (2011) *Short-Term Savings Equals Long-Term Problems for People with Autism.* Autism-Europe. Accessed 26 October 2015 at www.autismeurope.org/files/files/article-how-people-with-autism-are-affected-by-the-ongoing-financial-crisis.pdf.

Tony (2013) 'Anxious thoughts.' *Asperger United 76,* 4–5.

Tony (2015) 'Letter.' *Asperger United 83,* 11.

Trade Union Congress (2011) 'More disabled workers risk losing their jobs in public sector cut backs, warns TUC'. Press release, 21 January.

Trade Union Congress (2015) Trade Unions and Disabled Members: Why the Social Model Matters. TUC. Accessed 26 October 2015 at www.tuc.org.uk/sites/default/files/socialmodel.pdf.

Vallantyne, S. (2008) 'Surviving the Workplace: Asperger Syndrome for Employers.' In G. Edmonds and L. Beardon (eds) *Asperger Syndrome and Employment.* London: Jessica Kingsley Publishers.

Victoria (2014) 'Labels.' *Asperger United 79,* 4–5.

Walker, N. (2014a) 'Neurodiversity: Some Basic Terms and Definitions.' *Neurocosmopolitan.* Accessed 26 October 2015 at www.neurocosmopolitanism.com/neurodiversity-some-basic-terms-definitions.

Walker, N. (2014b) 'What is autism? The autistic view.' *The New Idealist: The Autism Issue 6,* 5.

Wheeler, E. (2015a) 'The right to speak up.' *Your Autism 49,* 1, 28–29.

Wheeler, E. (2015b) 'We are warriors.' *Your Autism 49,* 2, 25–26.

Worton, D. and Binks, P. (2008) 'Case Study by an Employee with Asperger Syndrome and His Line Manager.' In G. Edmonds and L. Beardon (eds) *Asperger Syndrome and Employment.* London: Jessica Kingsley Publishers.

Subject Index

Author Index